This book belongs to:

DOODLE

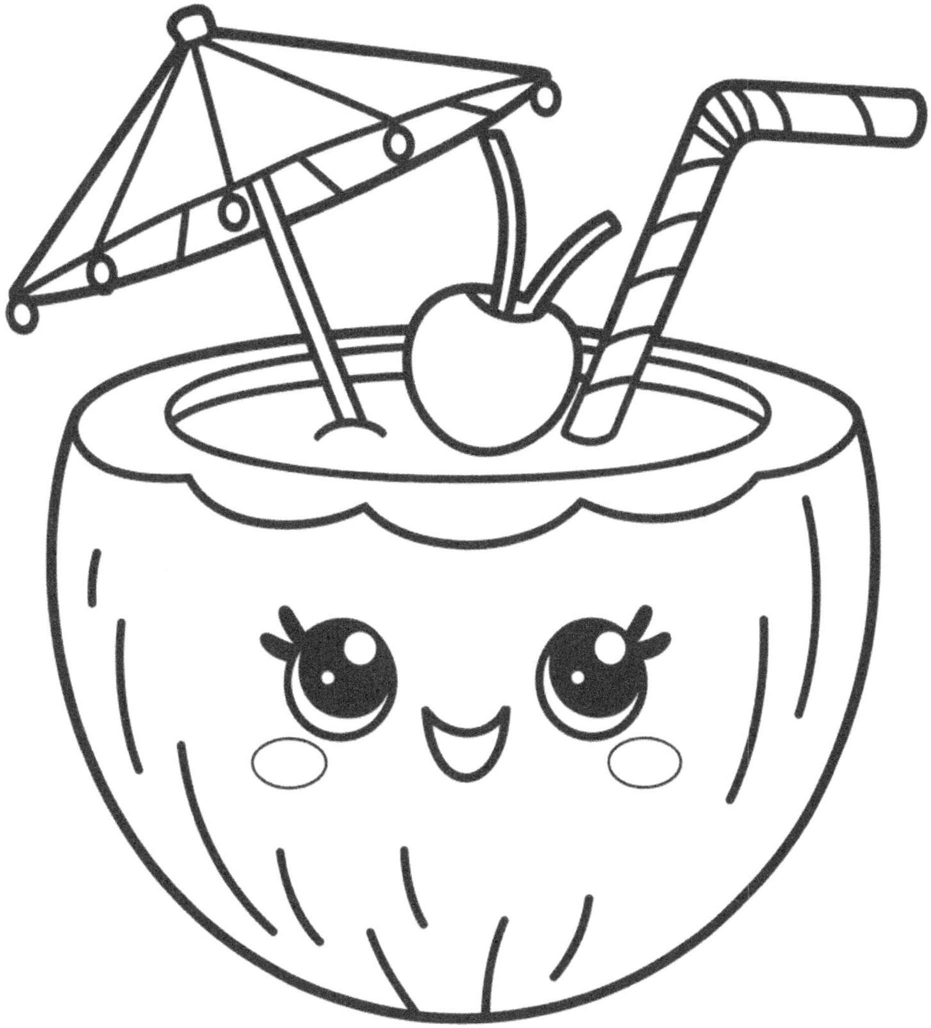

DOODLE

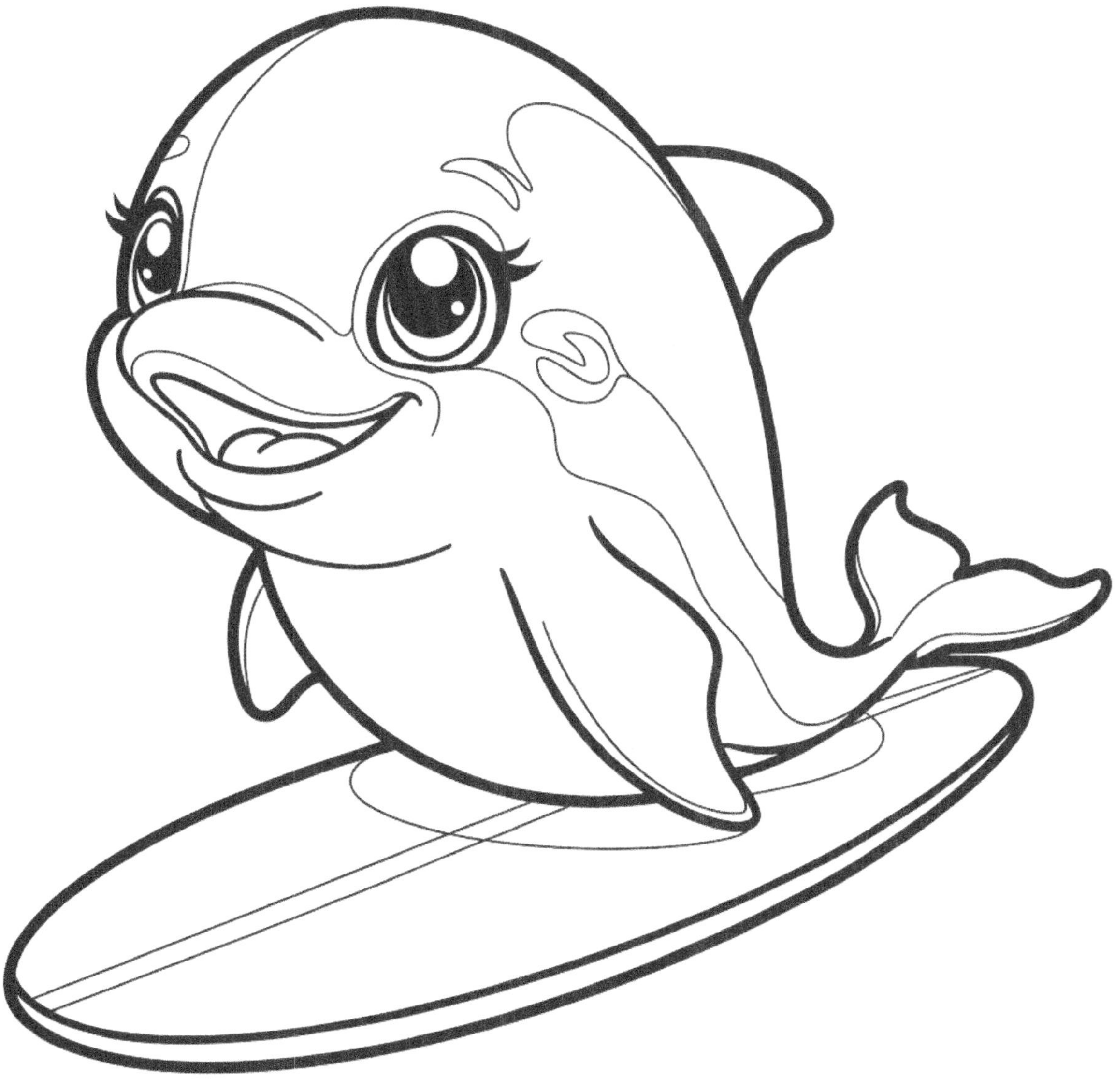

DOODLE

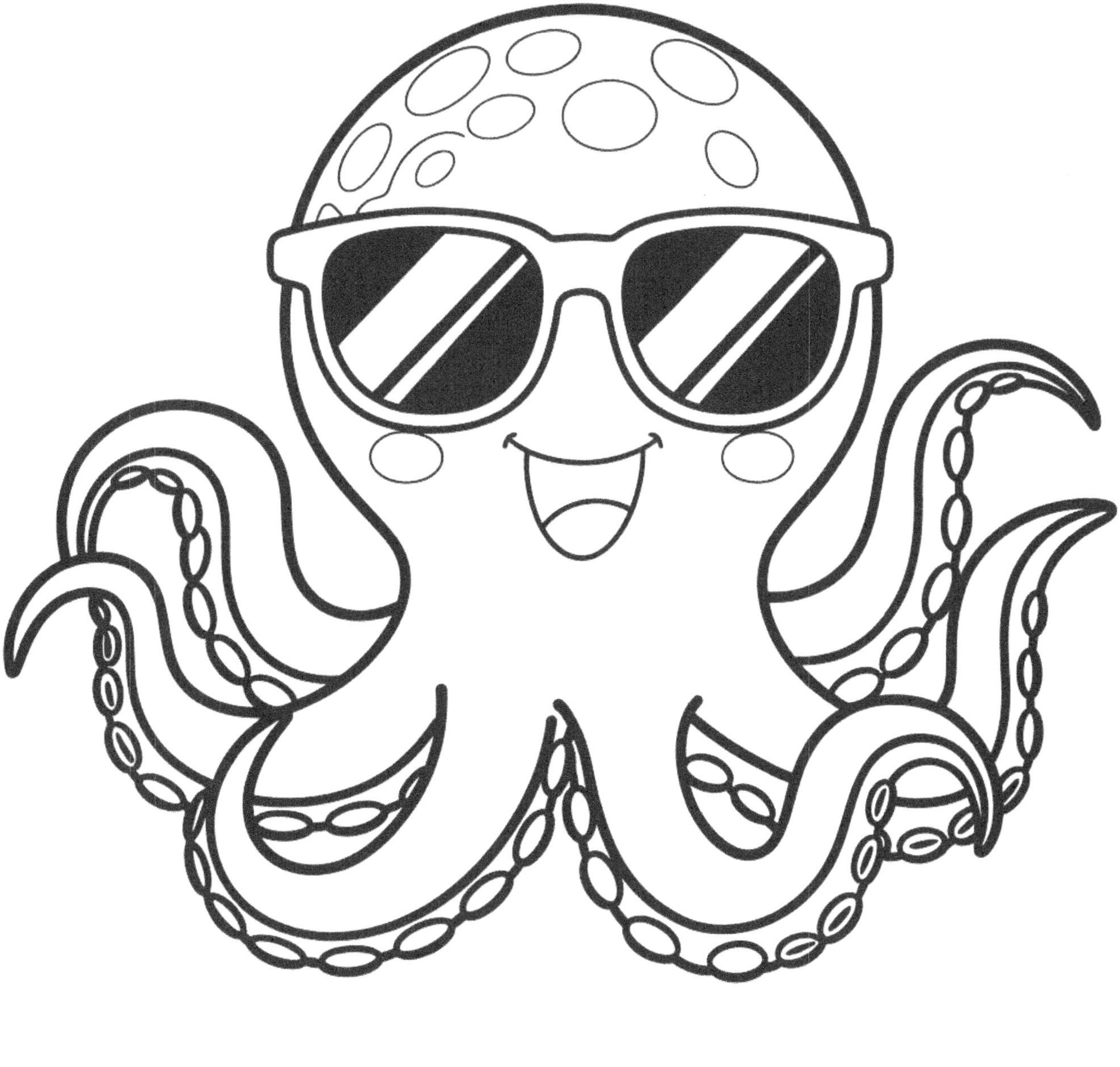

DOODLE

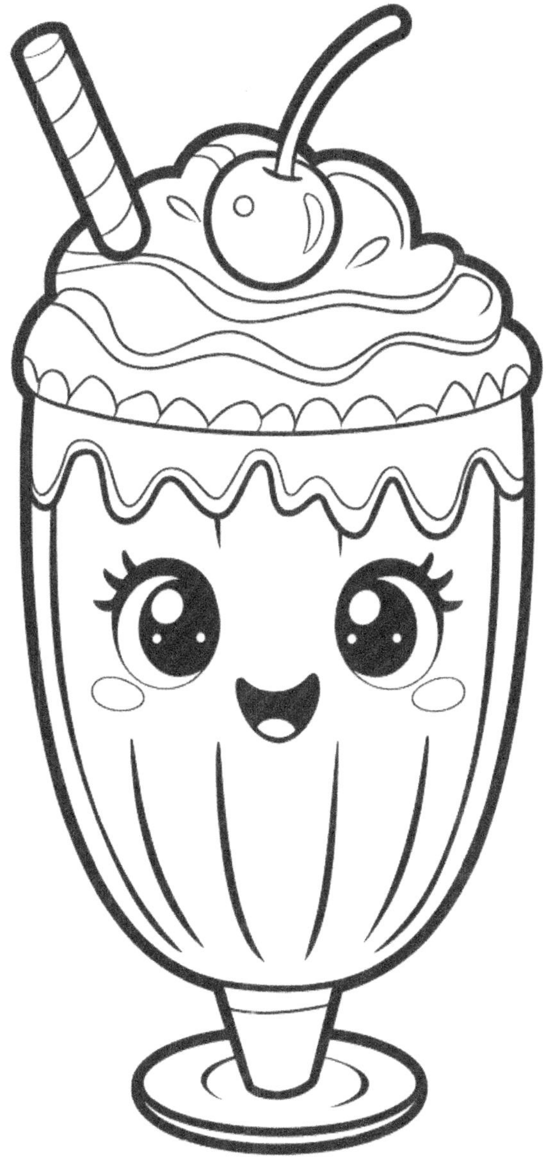

DOODLE

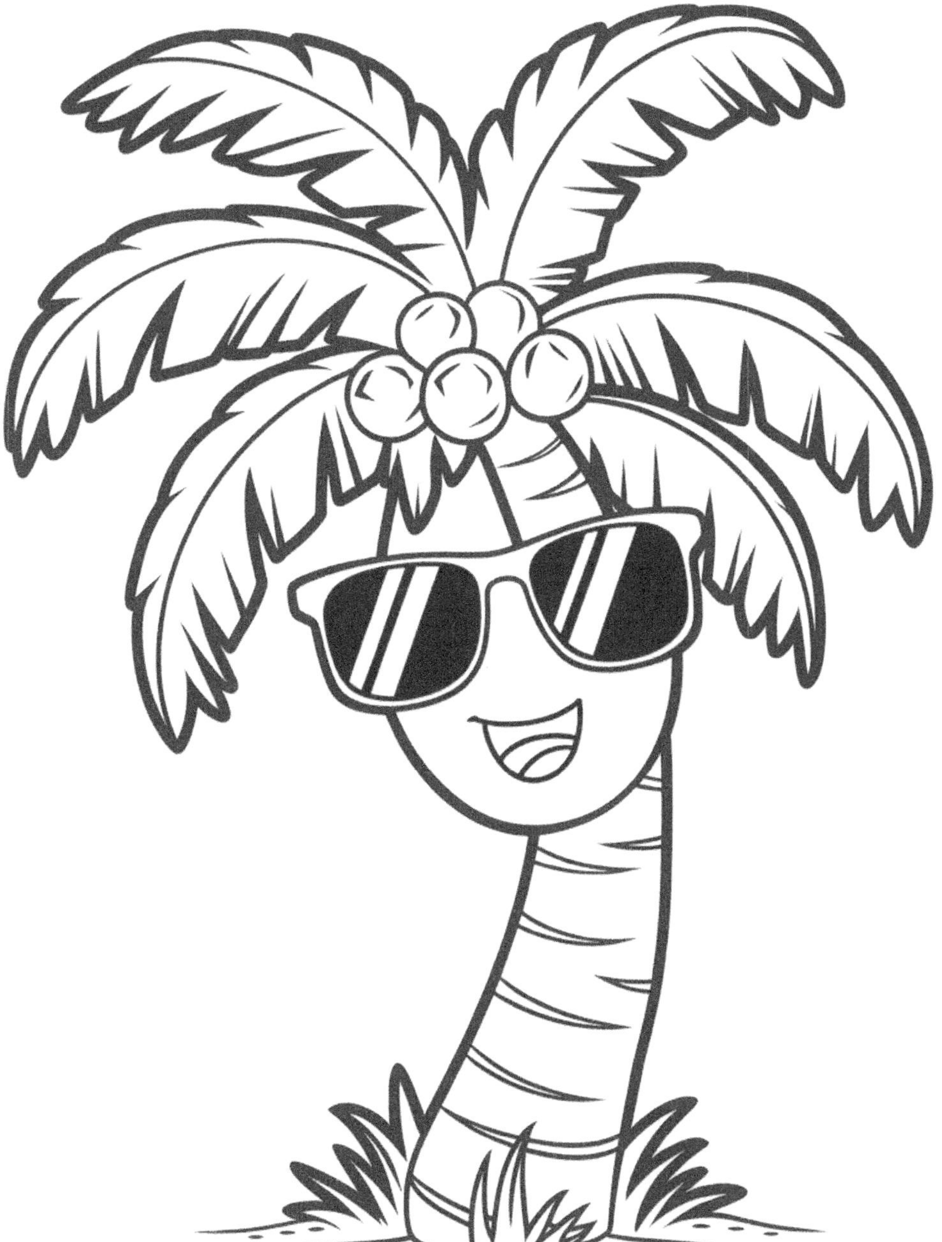

DOODLE

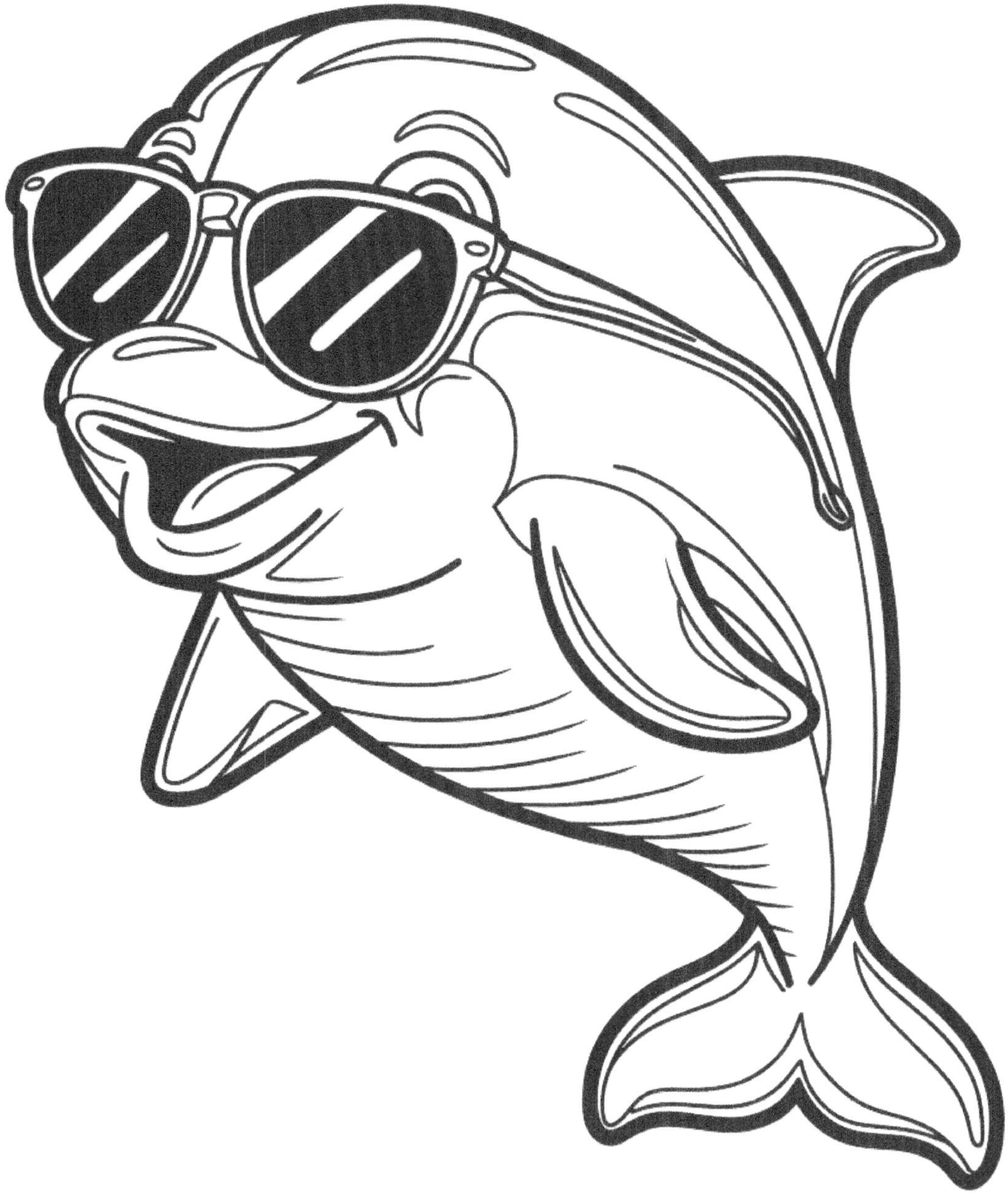

DOODLE

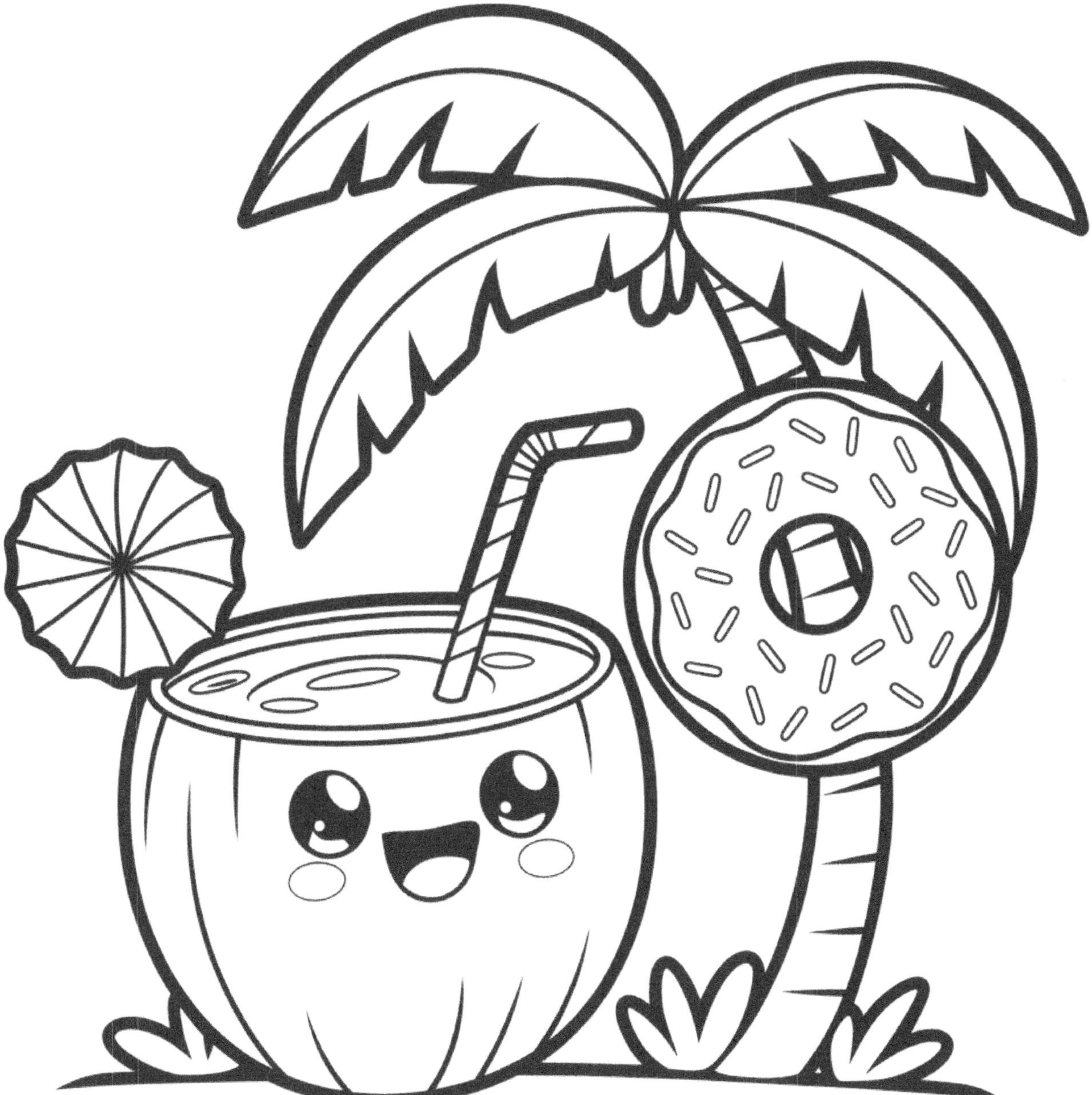

DOODLE

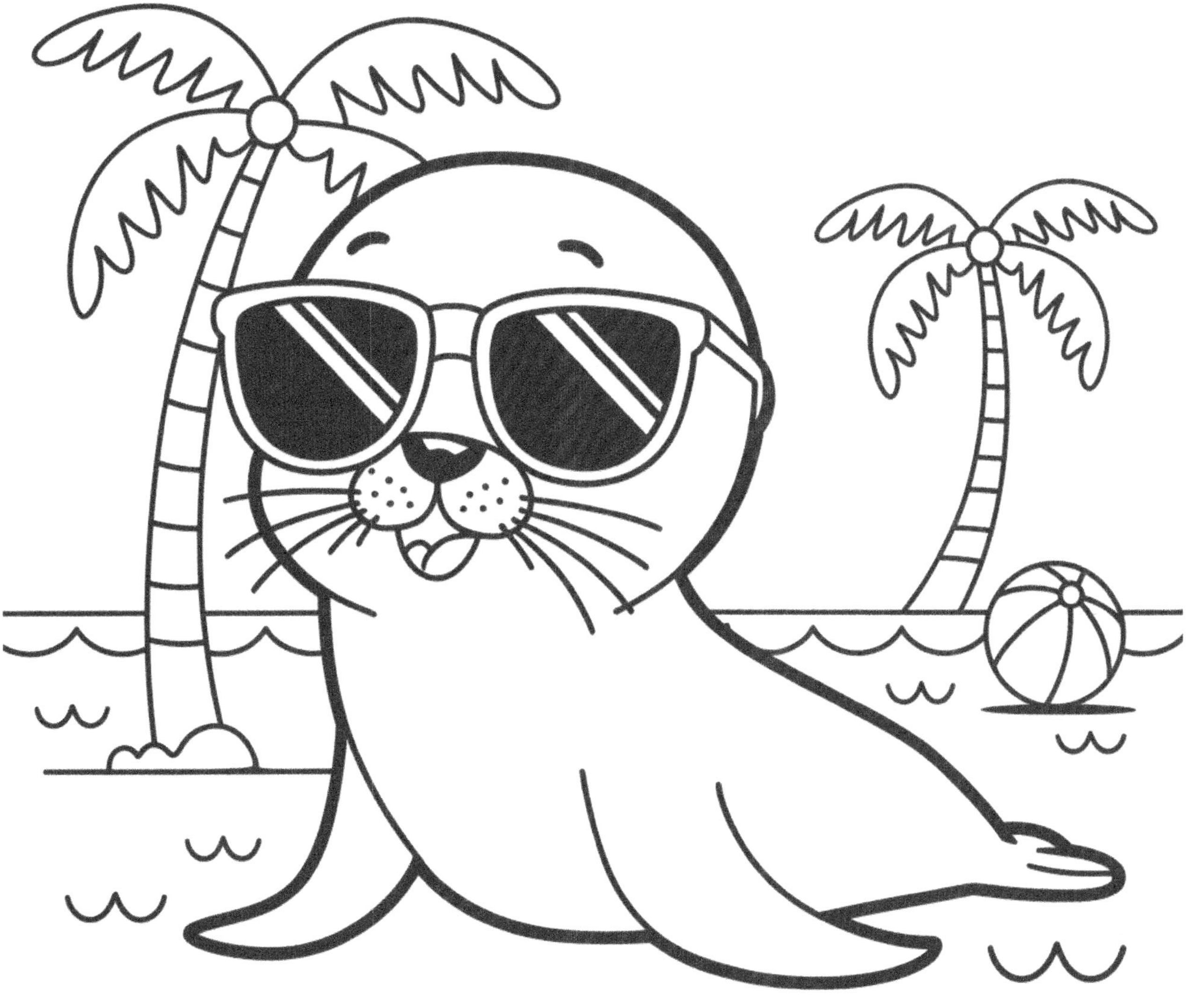

DOODLE

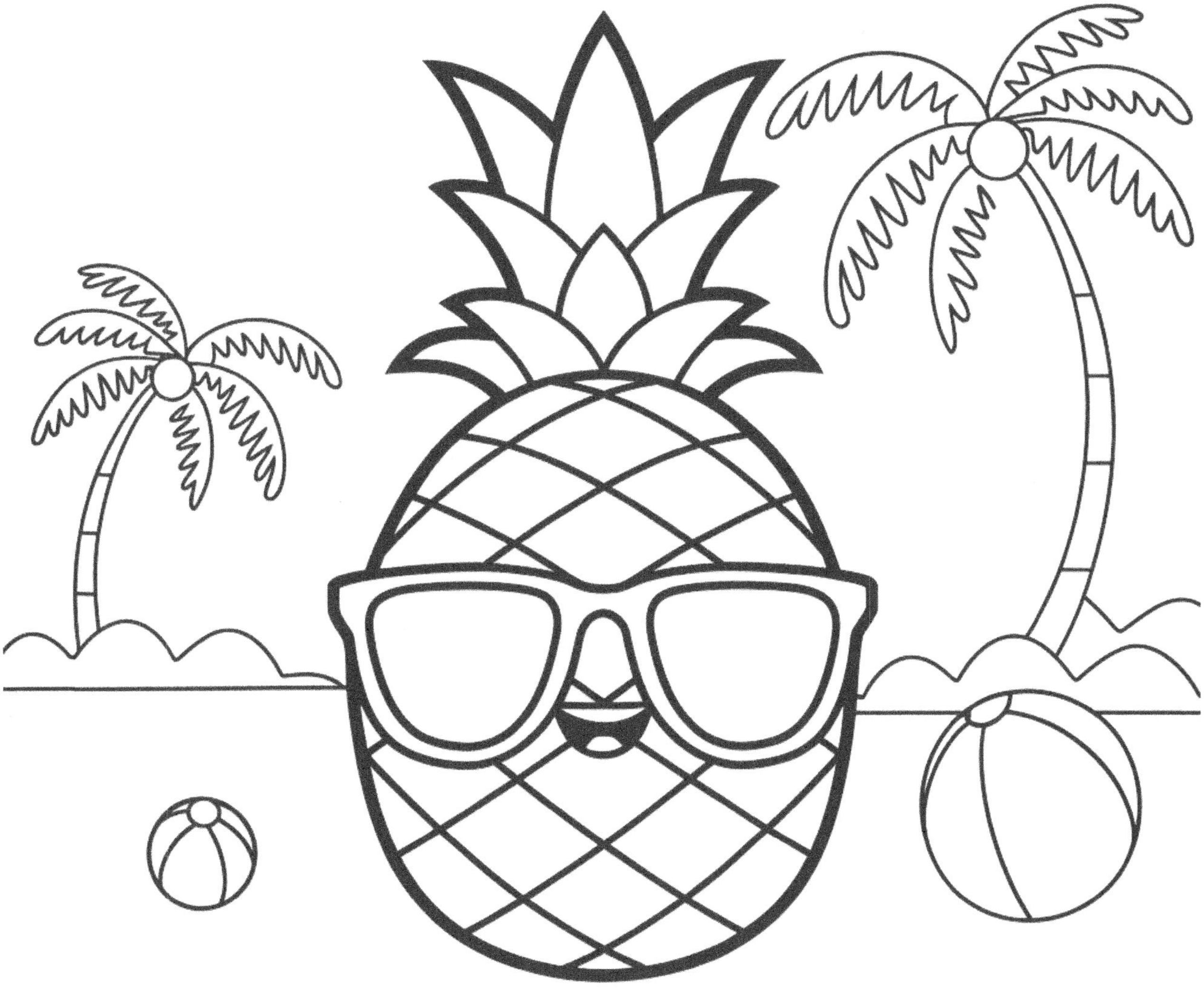

DOODLE

OCEAN STARS

DOODLE

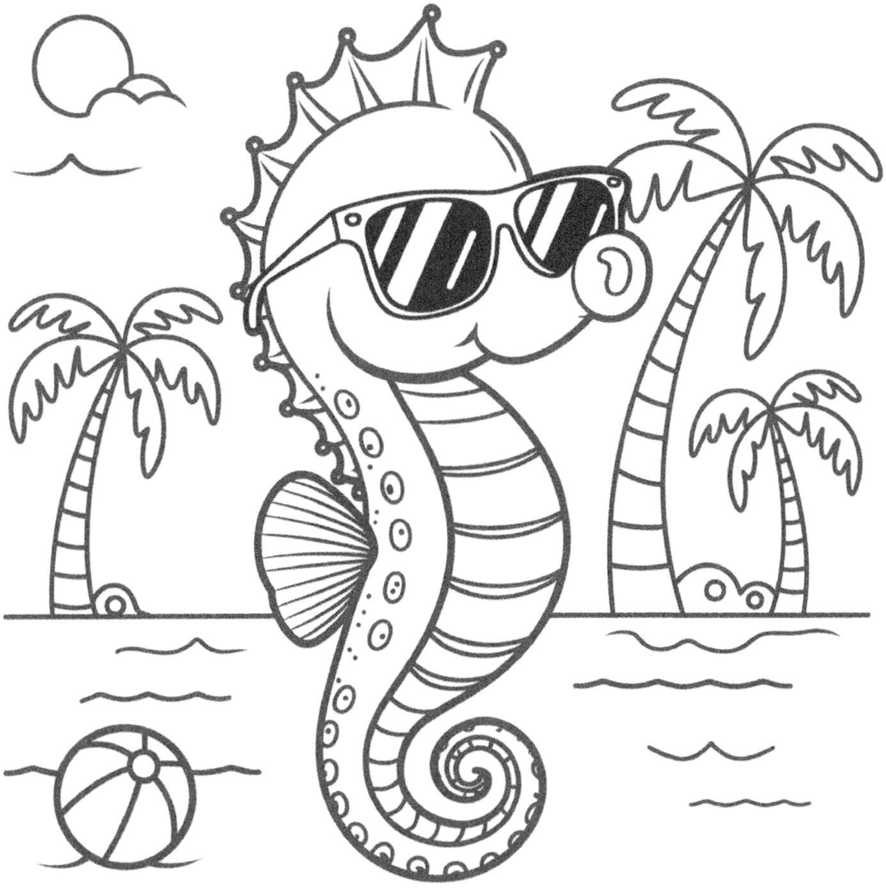

DOODLE

HAWAII FRIENDS

DOODLE

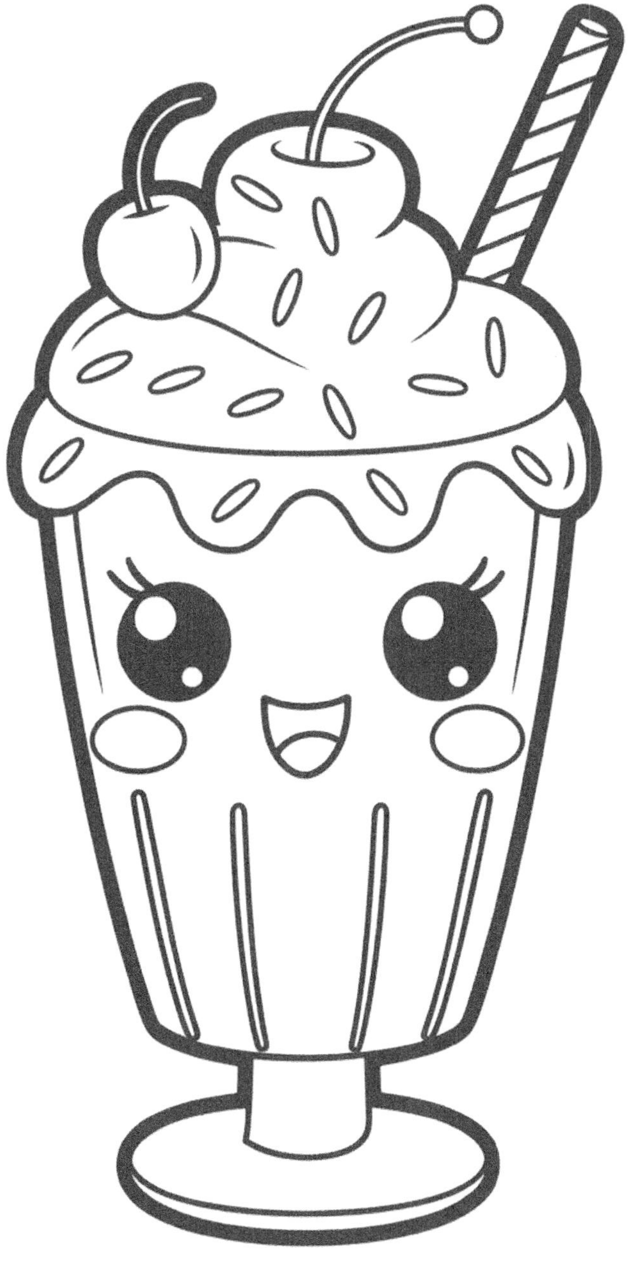

DOODLE

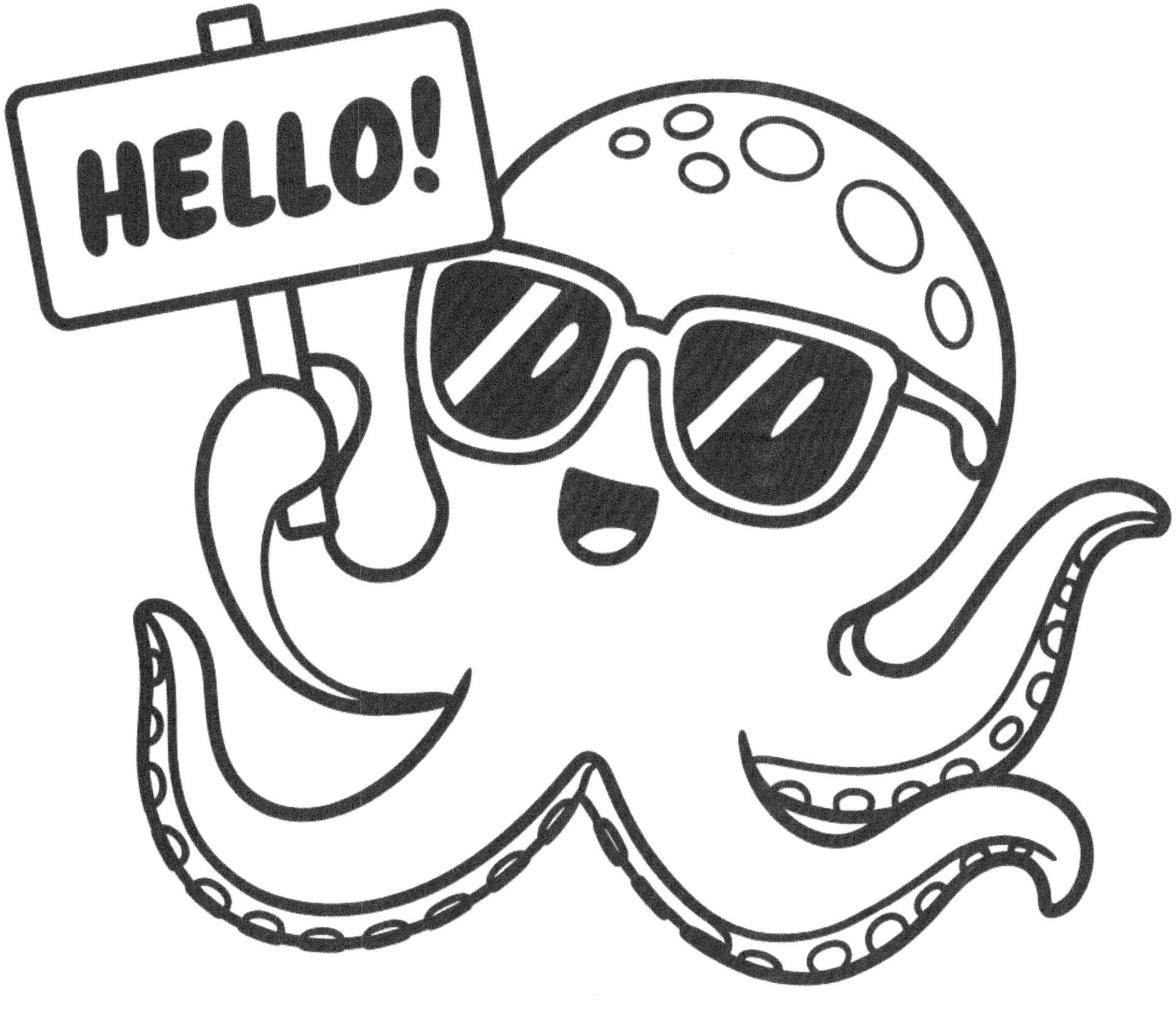
HELLO!

DOODLE

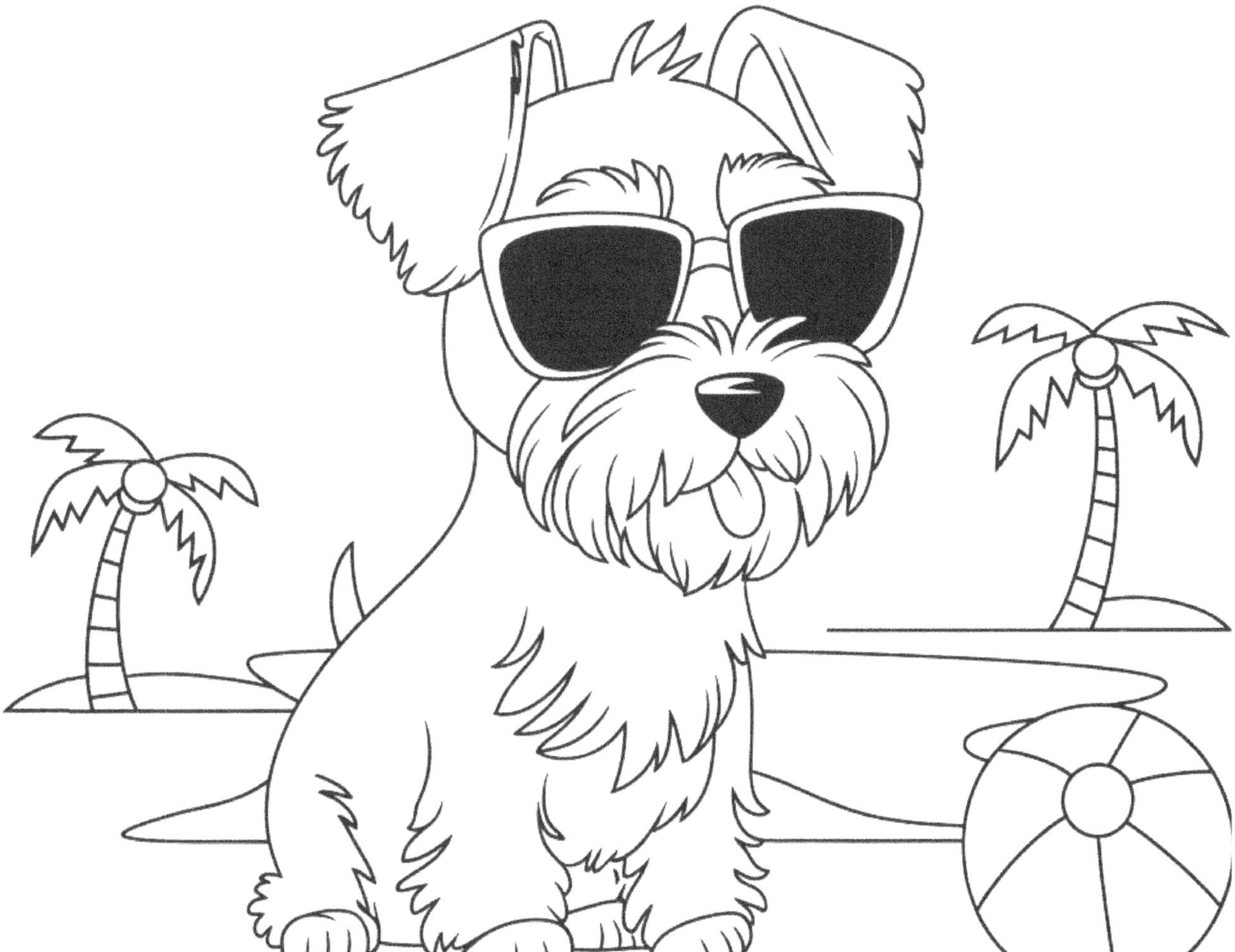

DOODLE

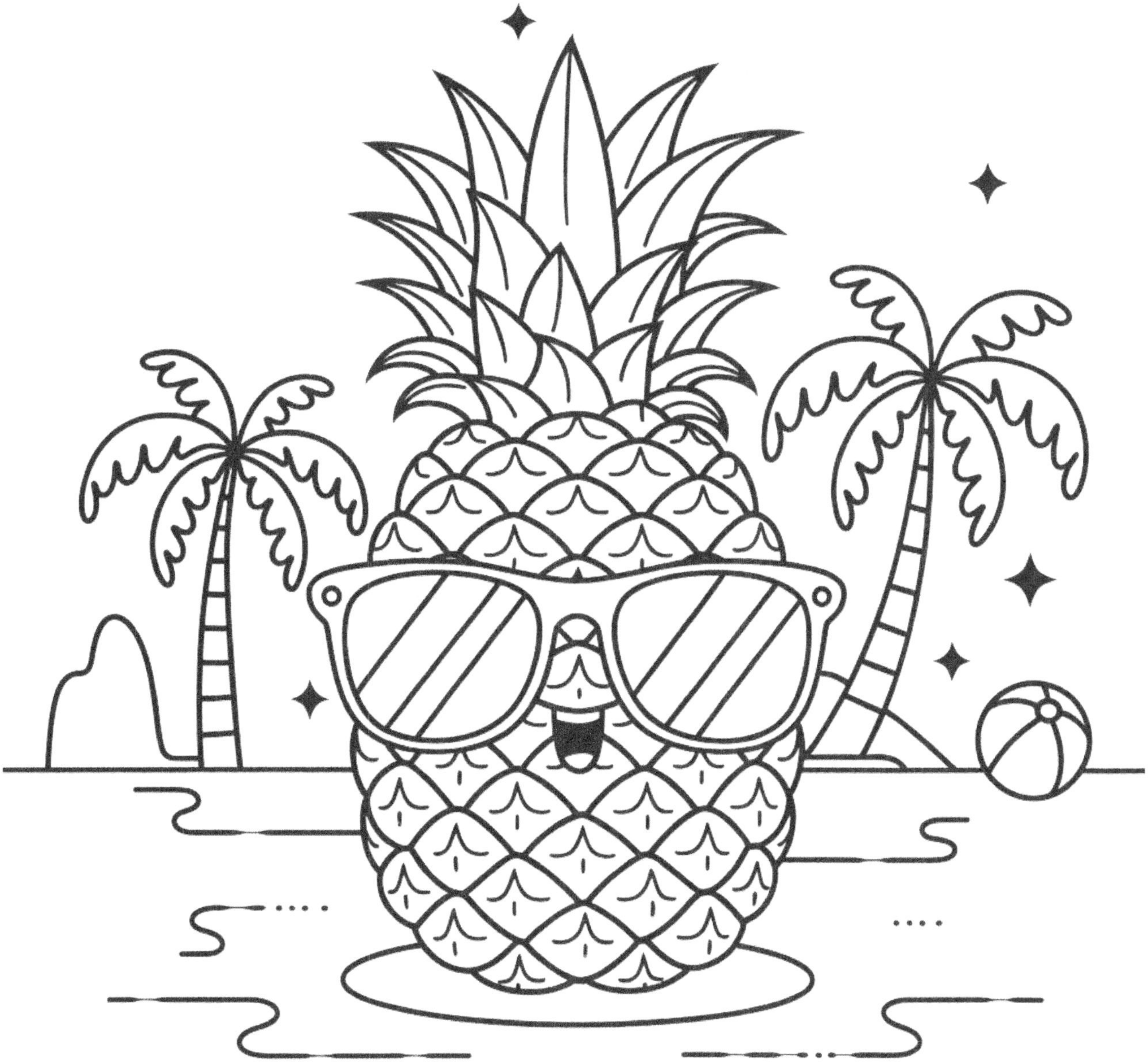

DOODLE

BURGERS ON THE BEACH

DOODLE

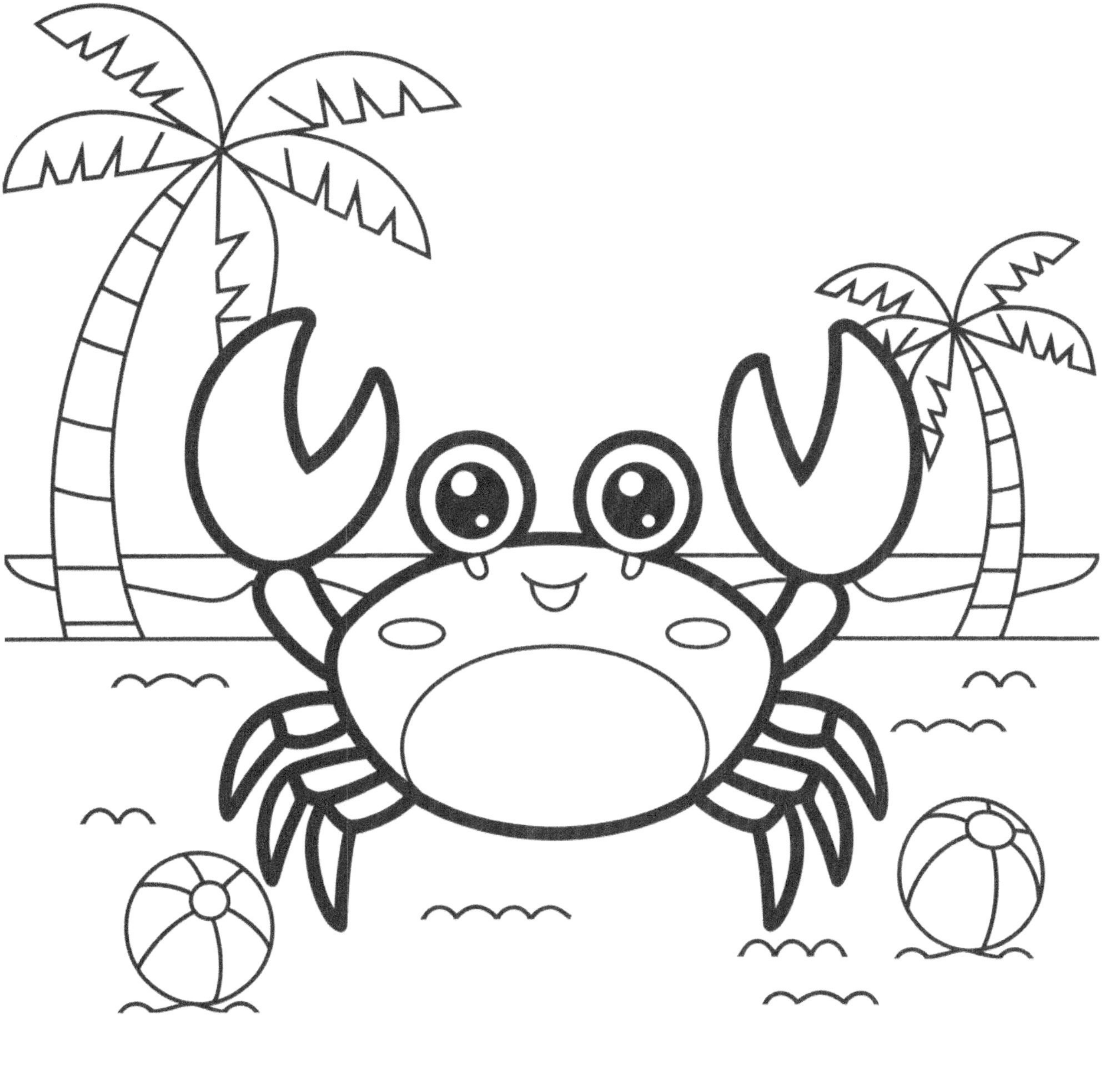

DOODLE

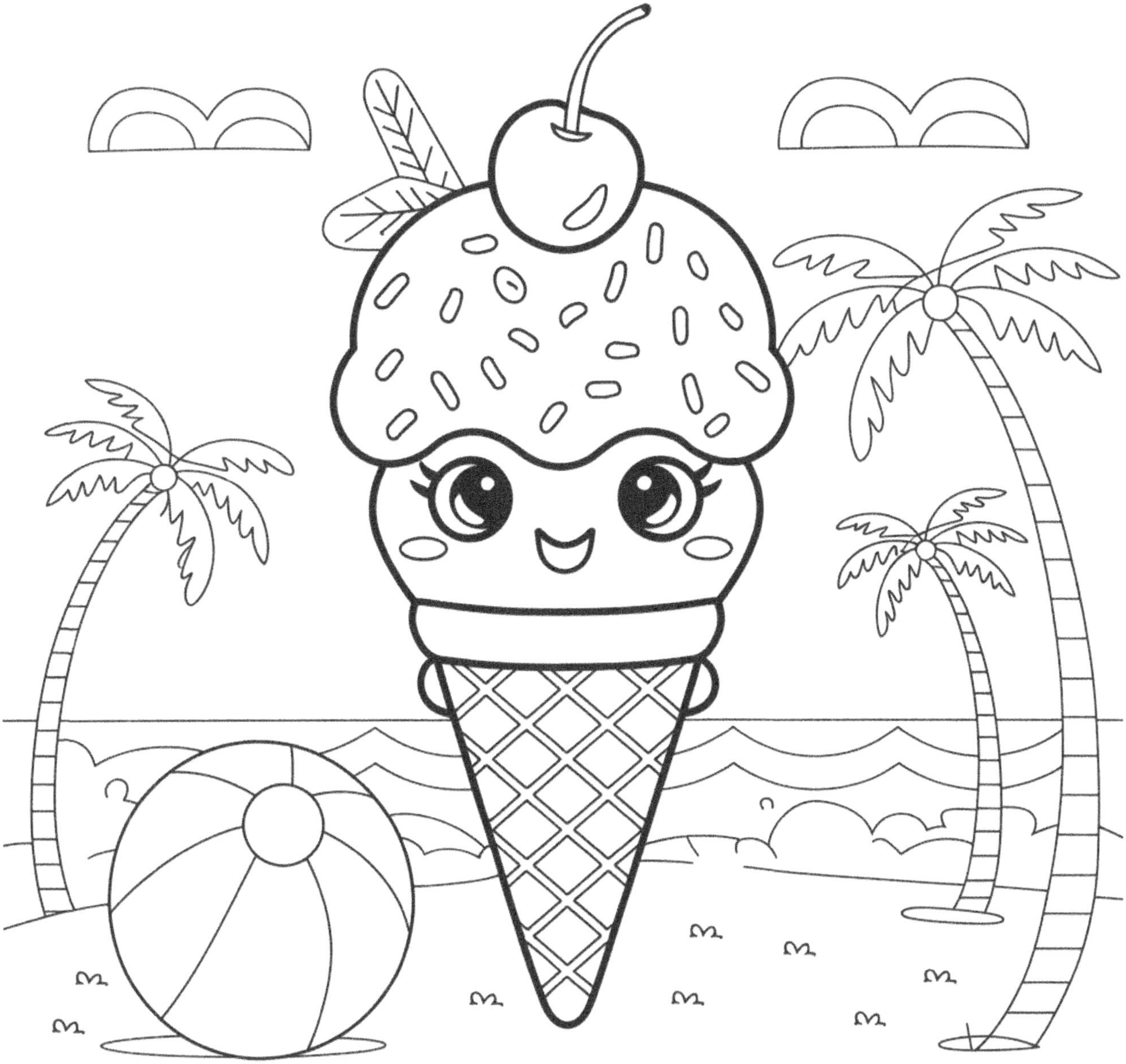

DOODLE

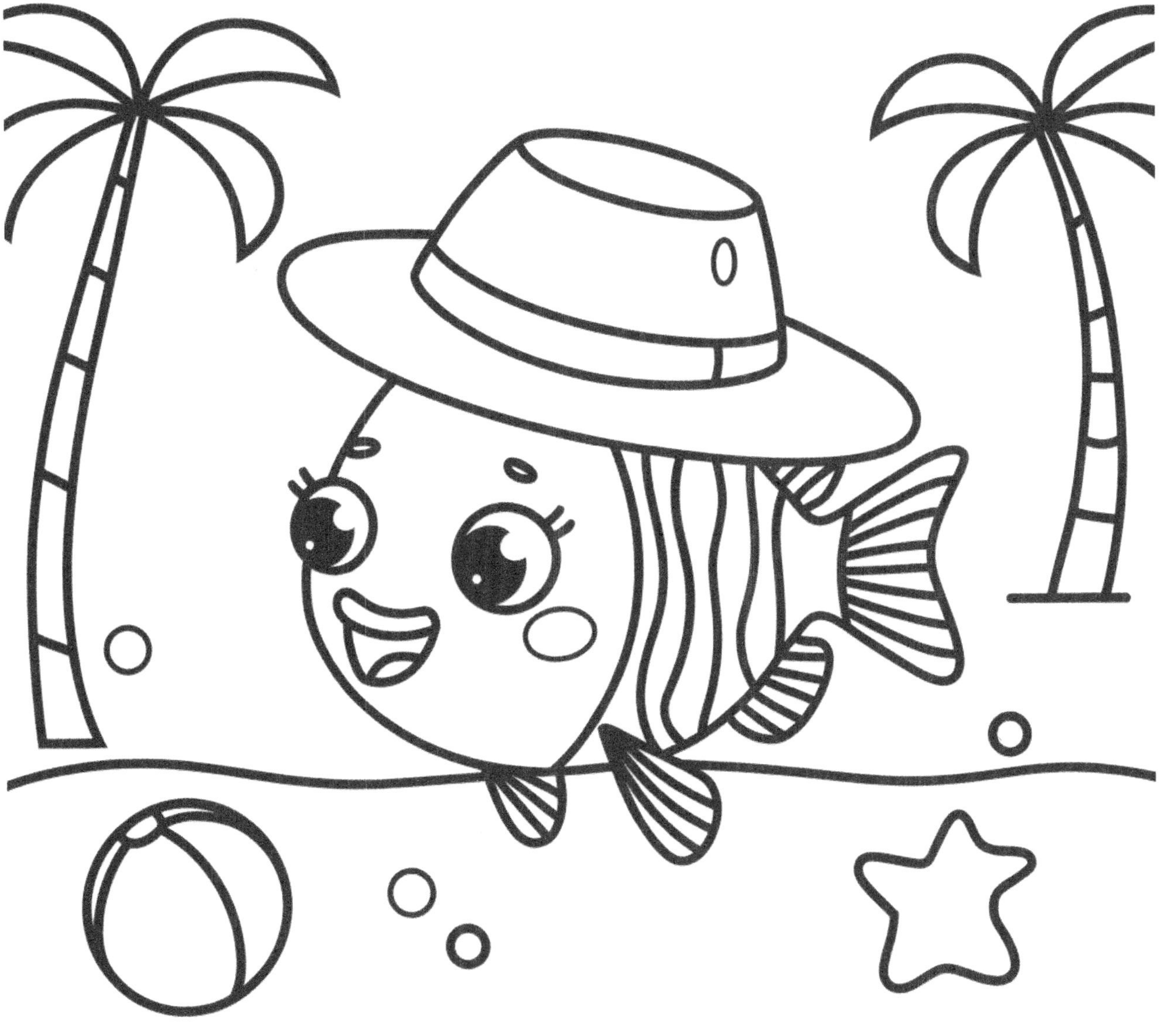

DOODLE

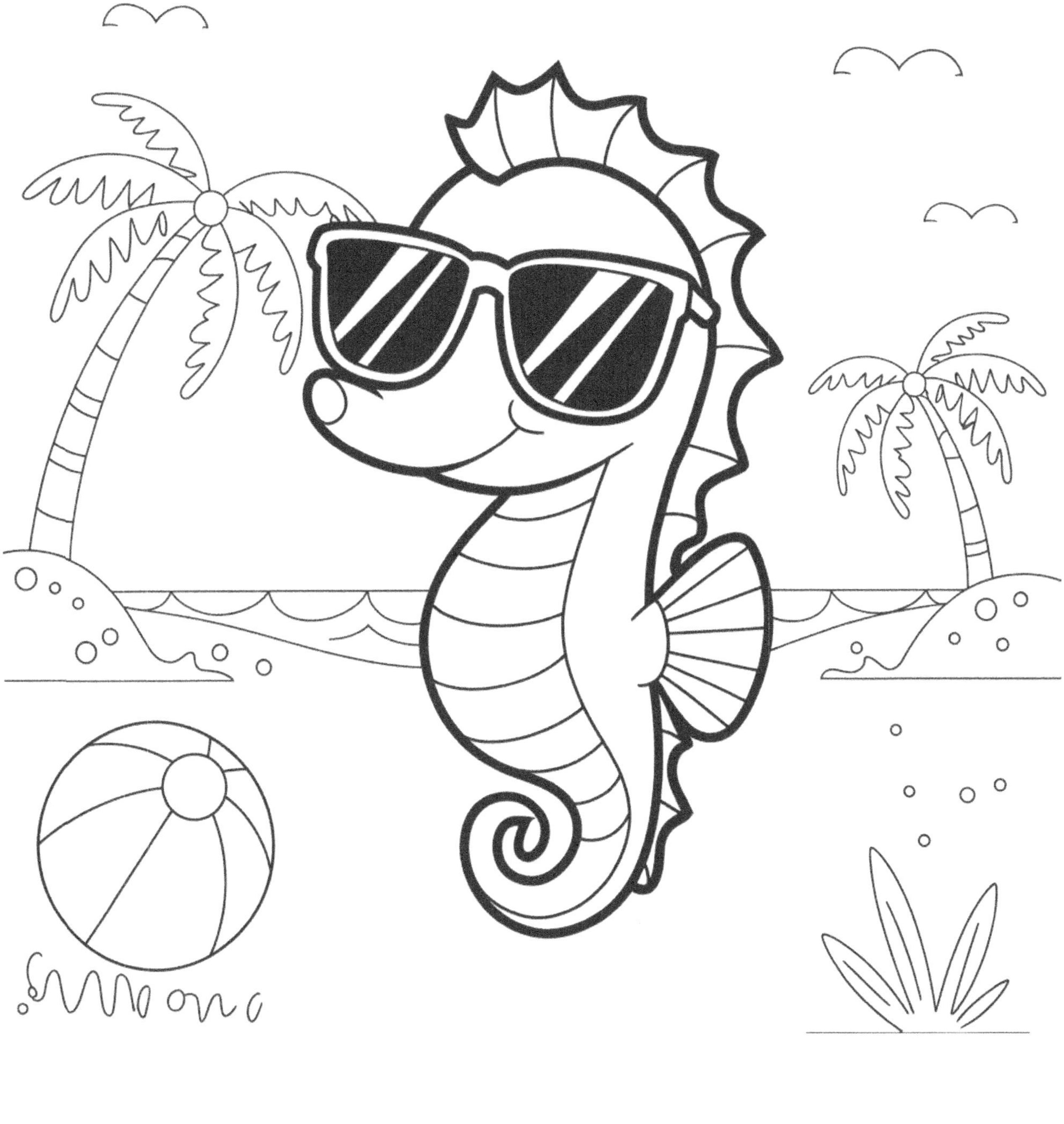

DOODLE

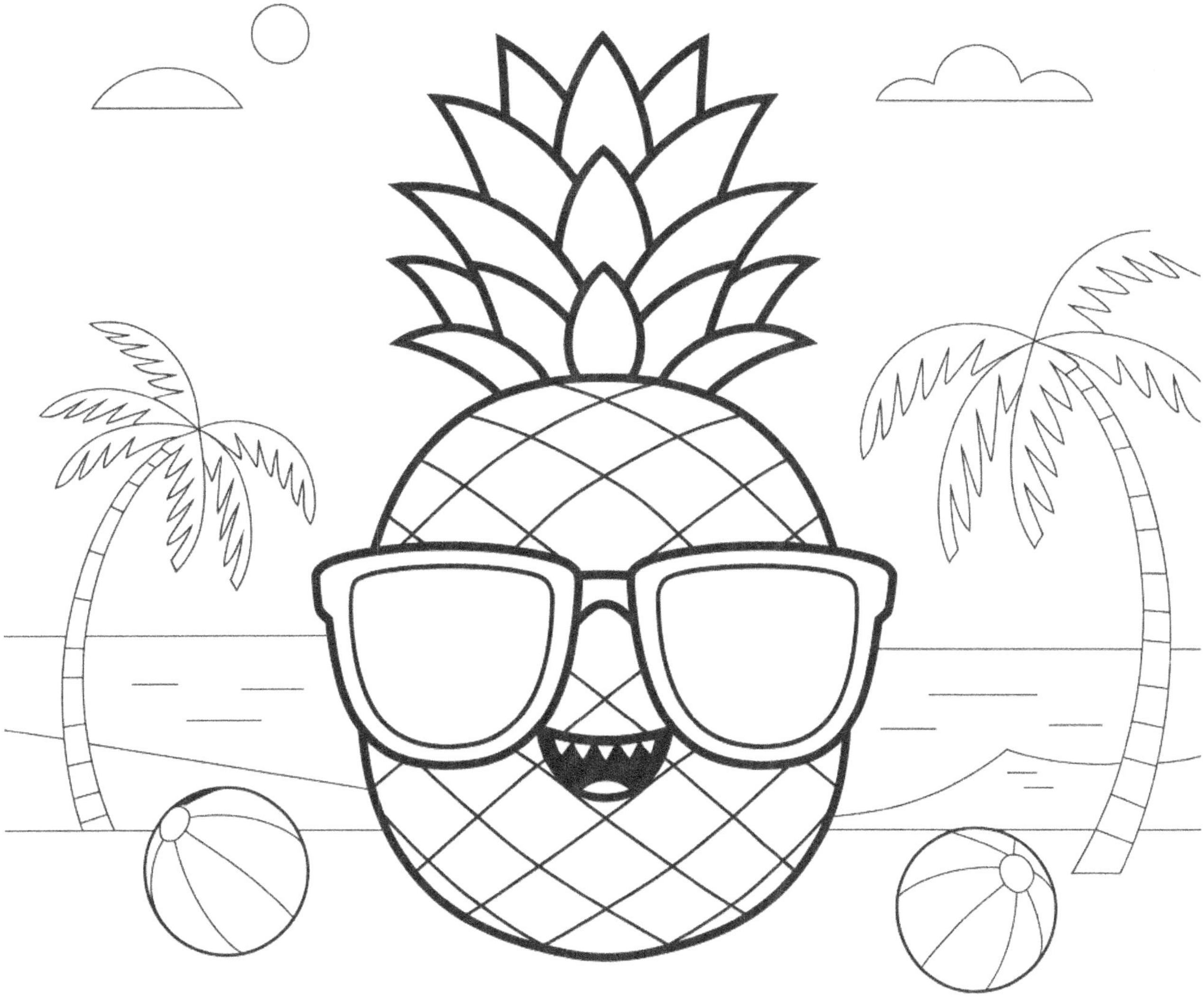

DOODLE

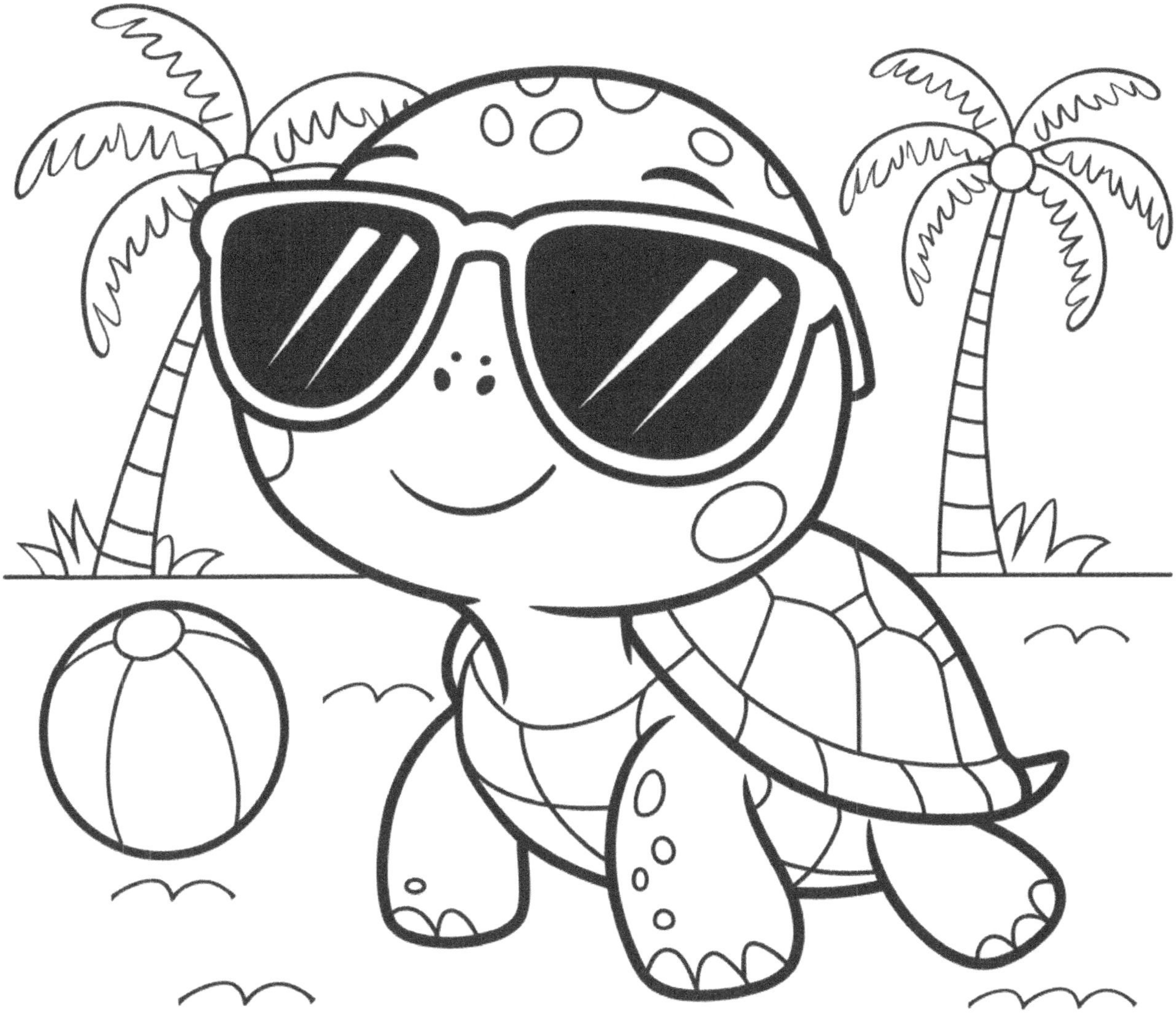

DOODLE

SWEET
FRIENDS

DOODLE

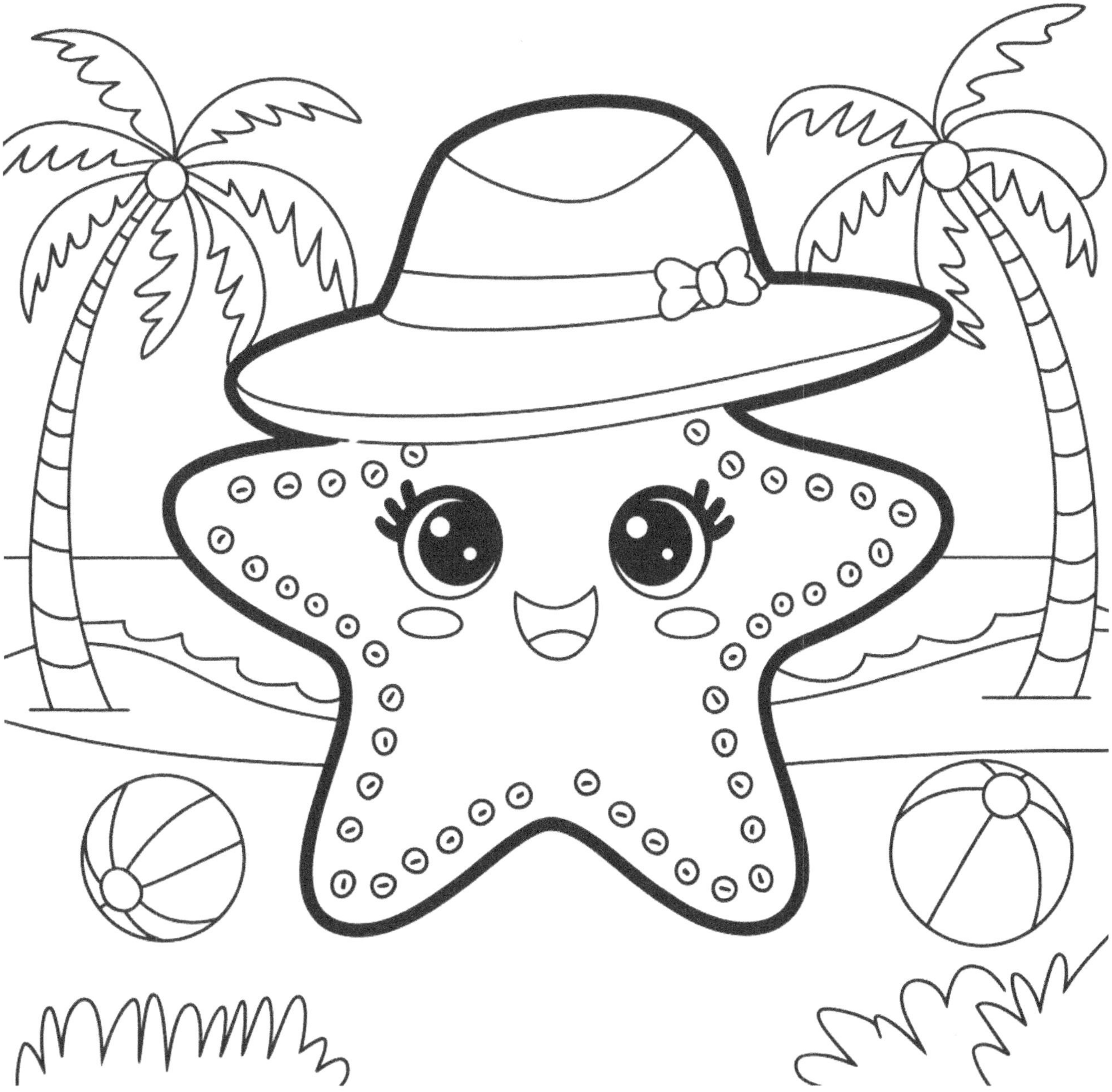

DOODLE

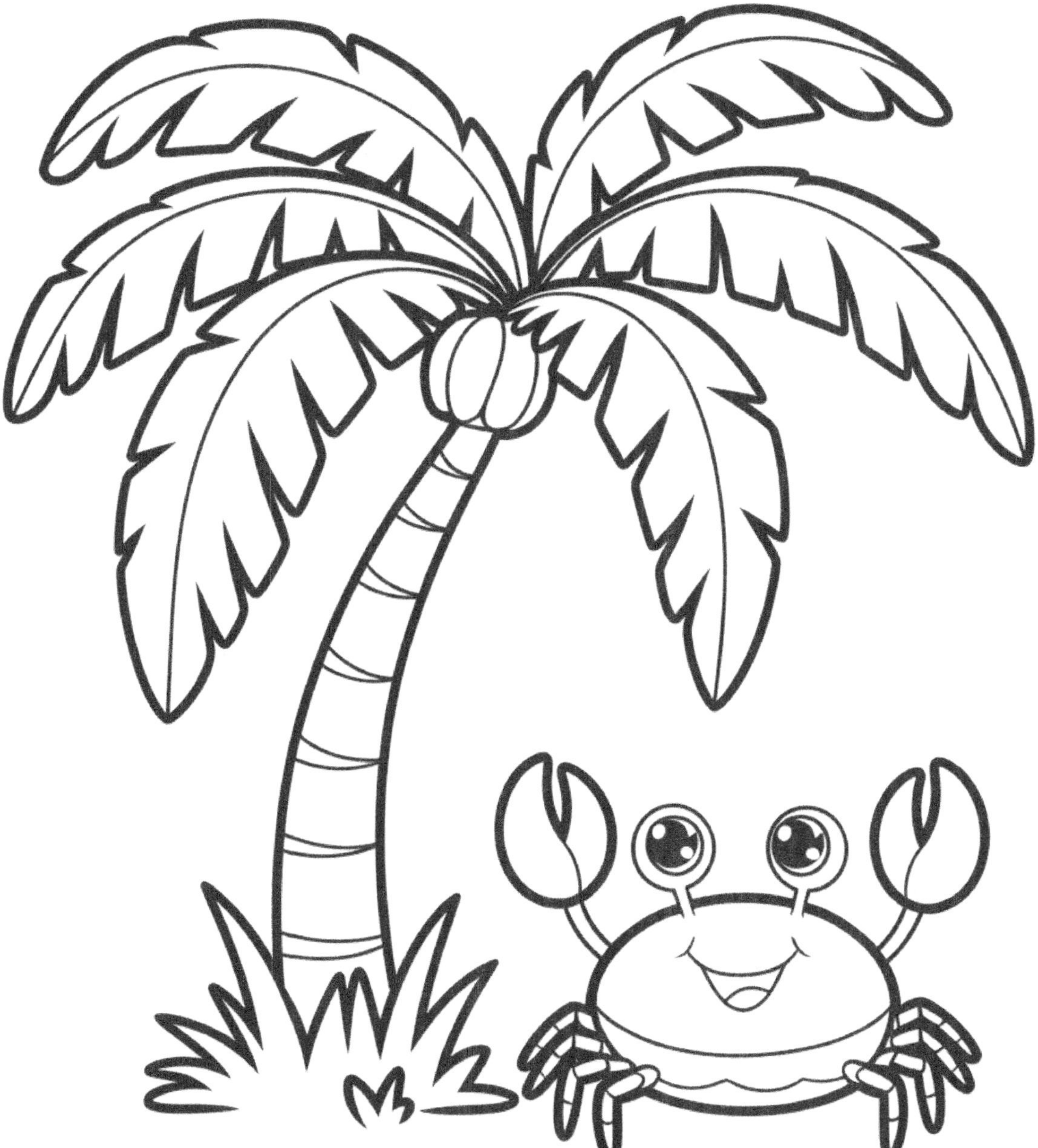

DOODLE

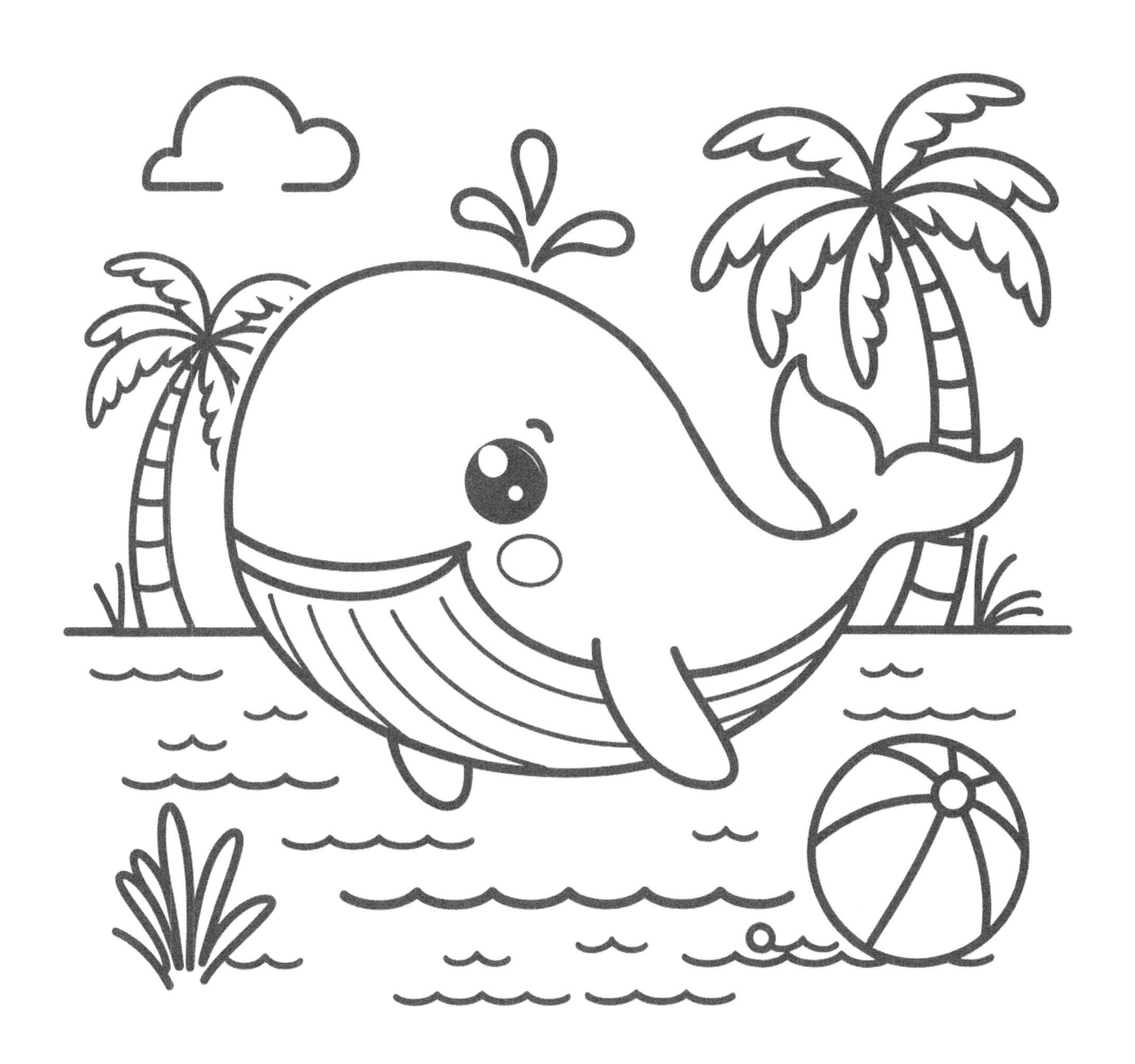

DOODLE

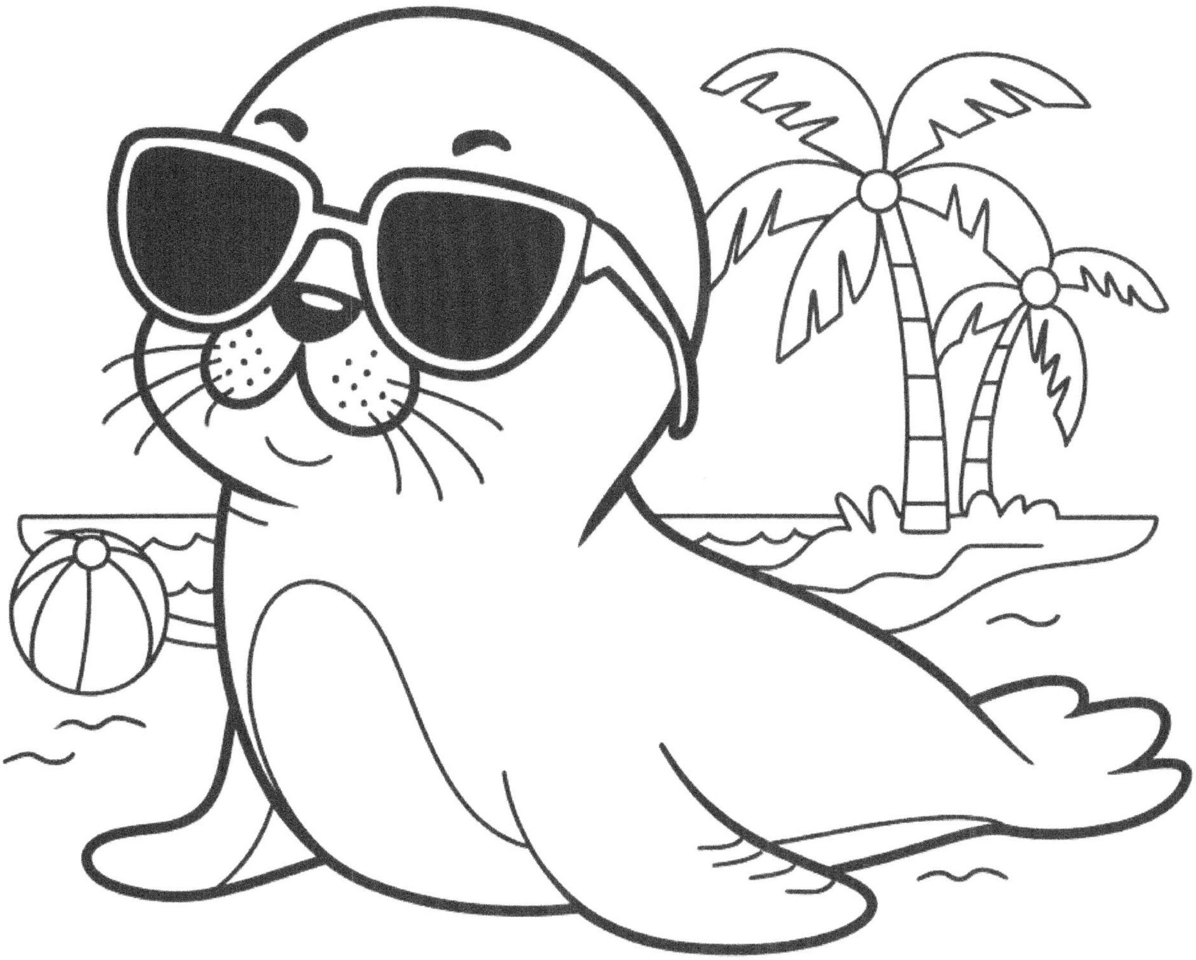

DOODLE

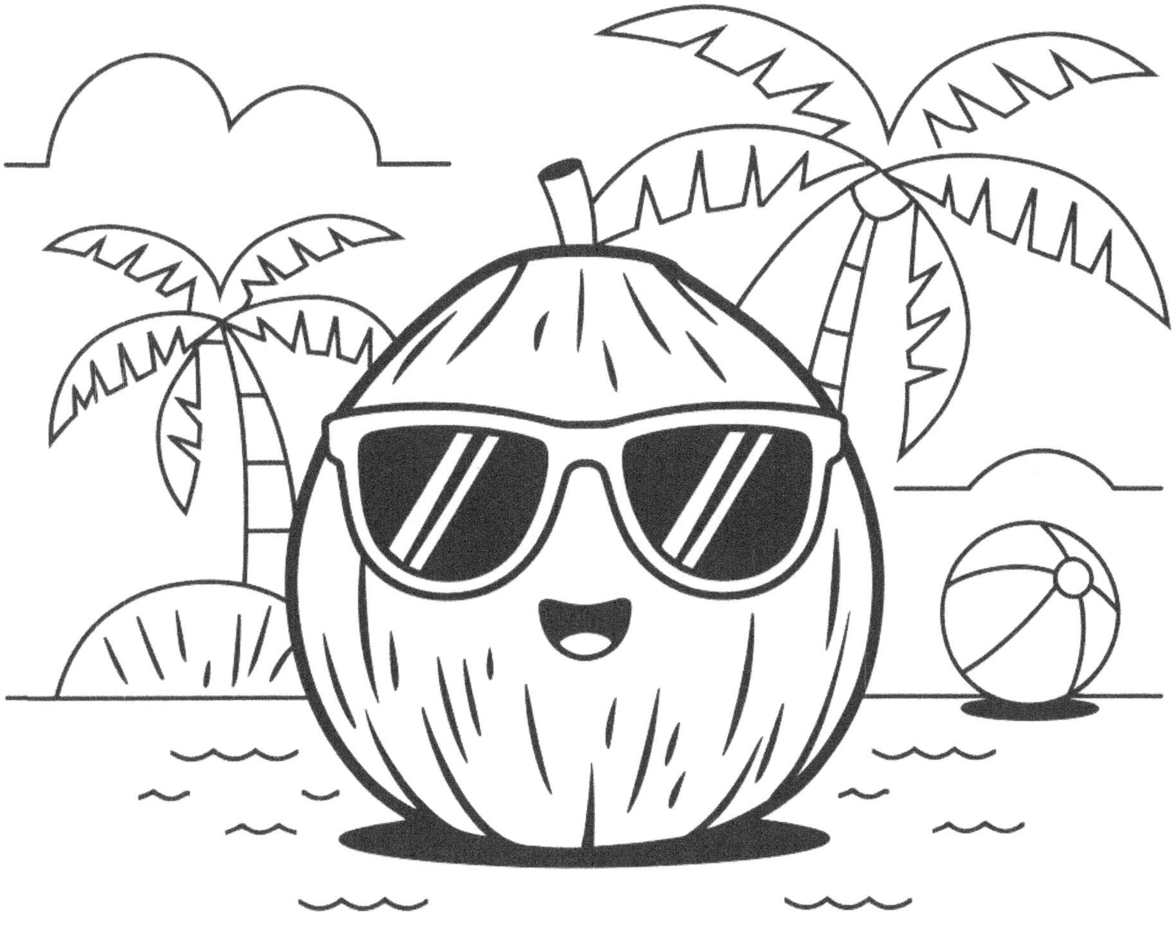

DOODLE

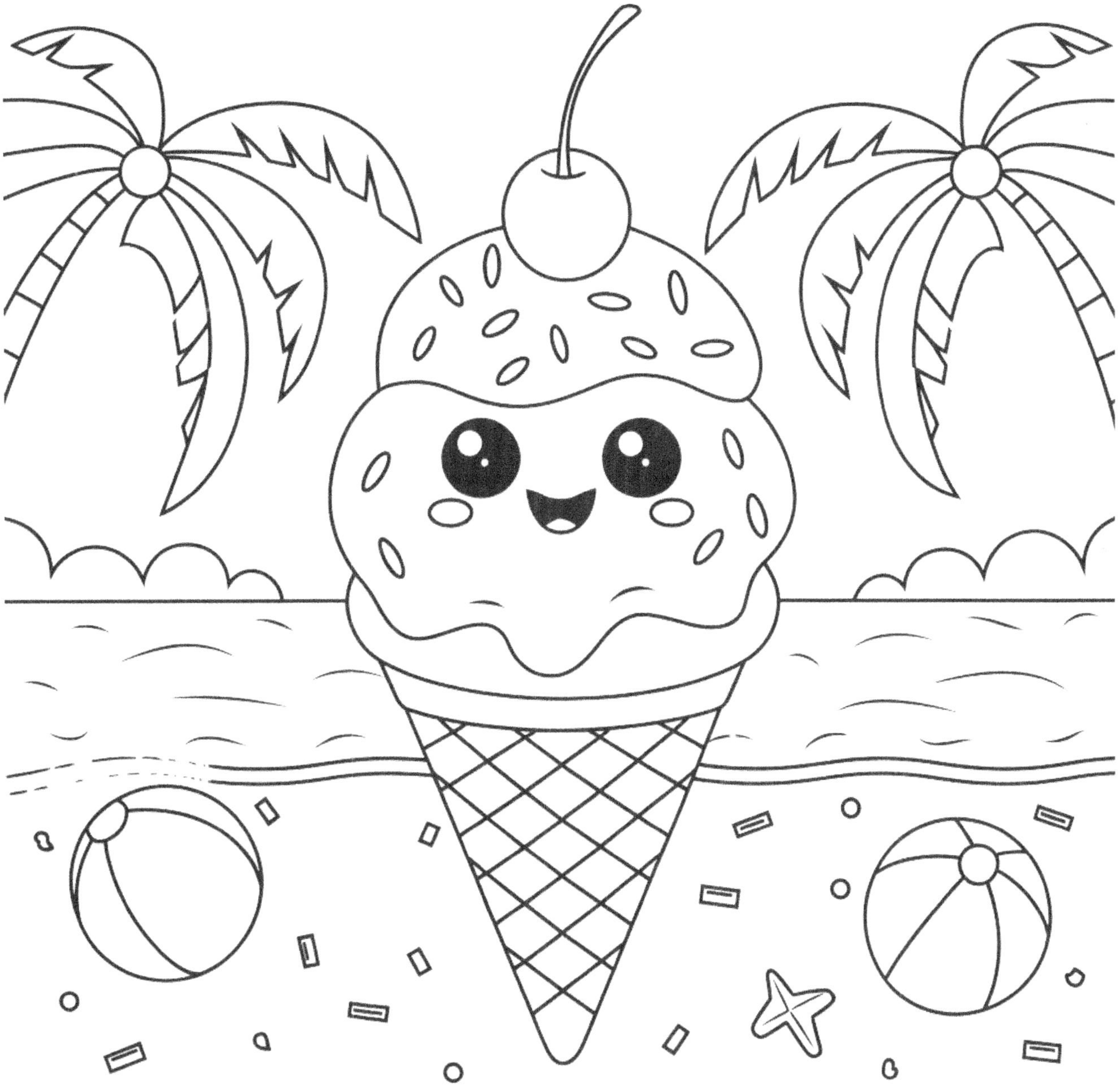

DOODLE

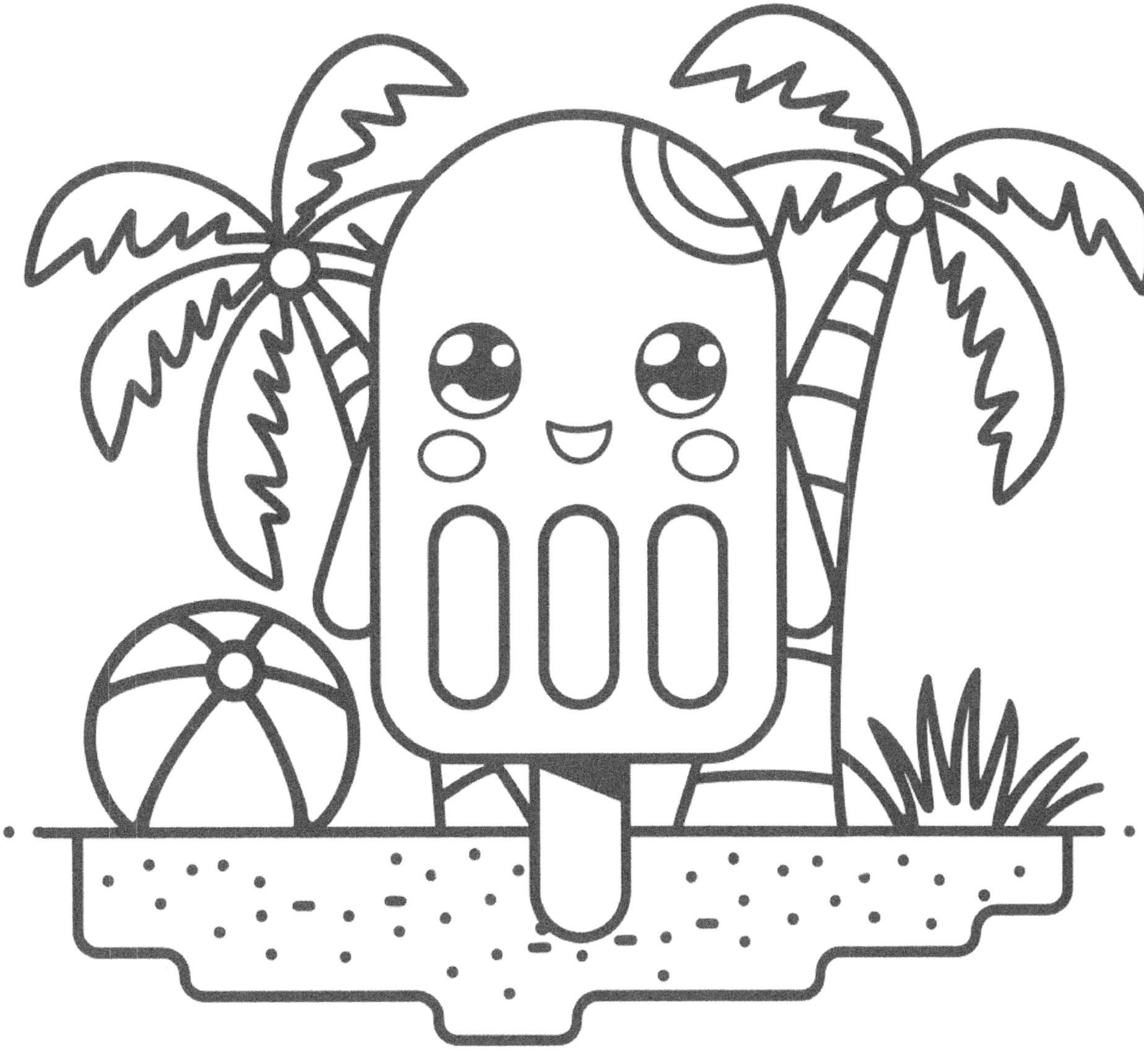

DOODLE

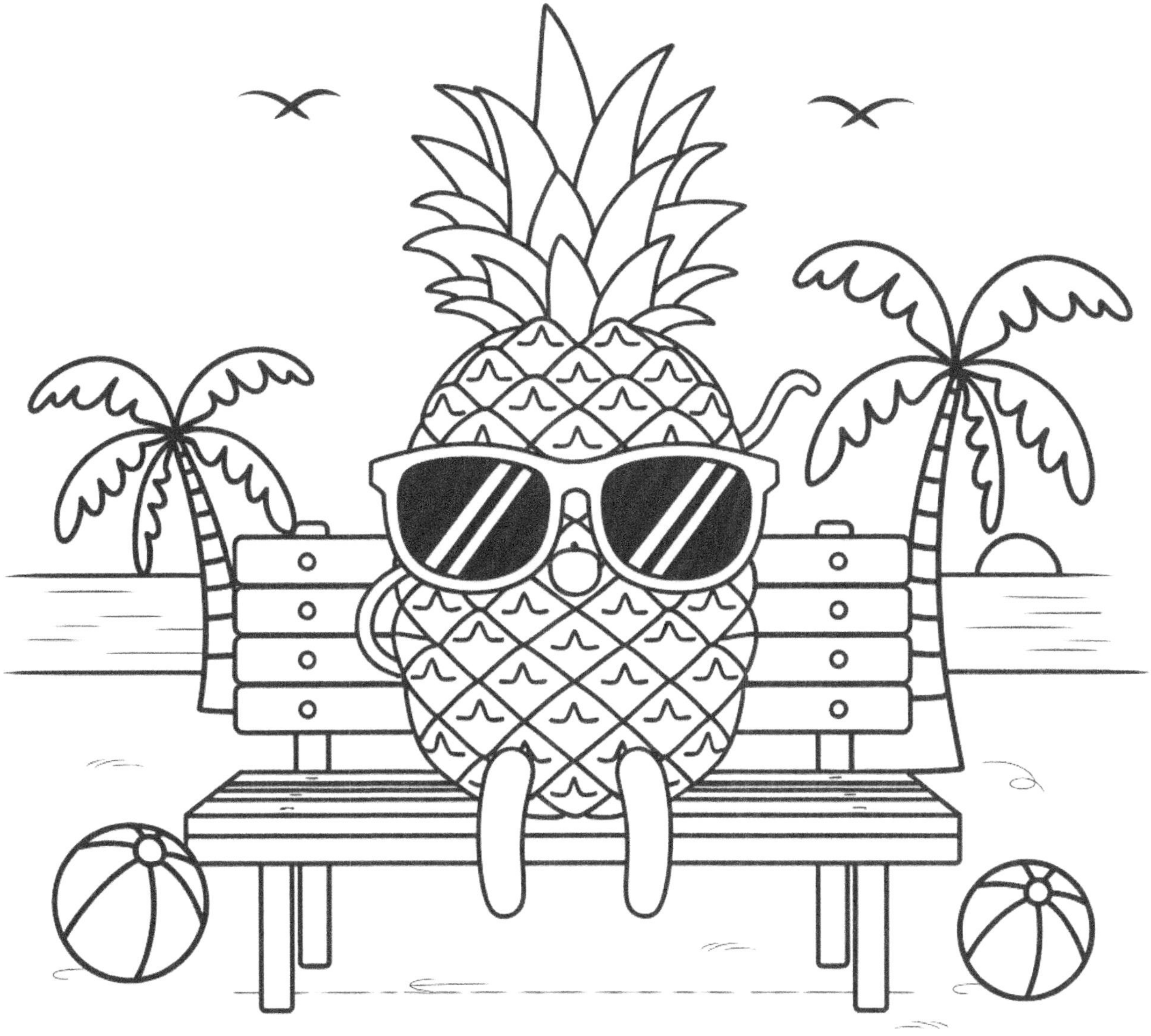

DOODLE

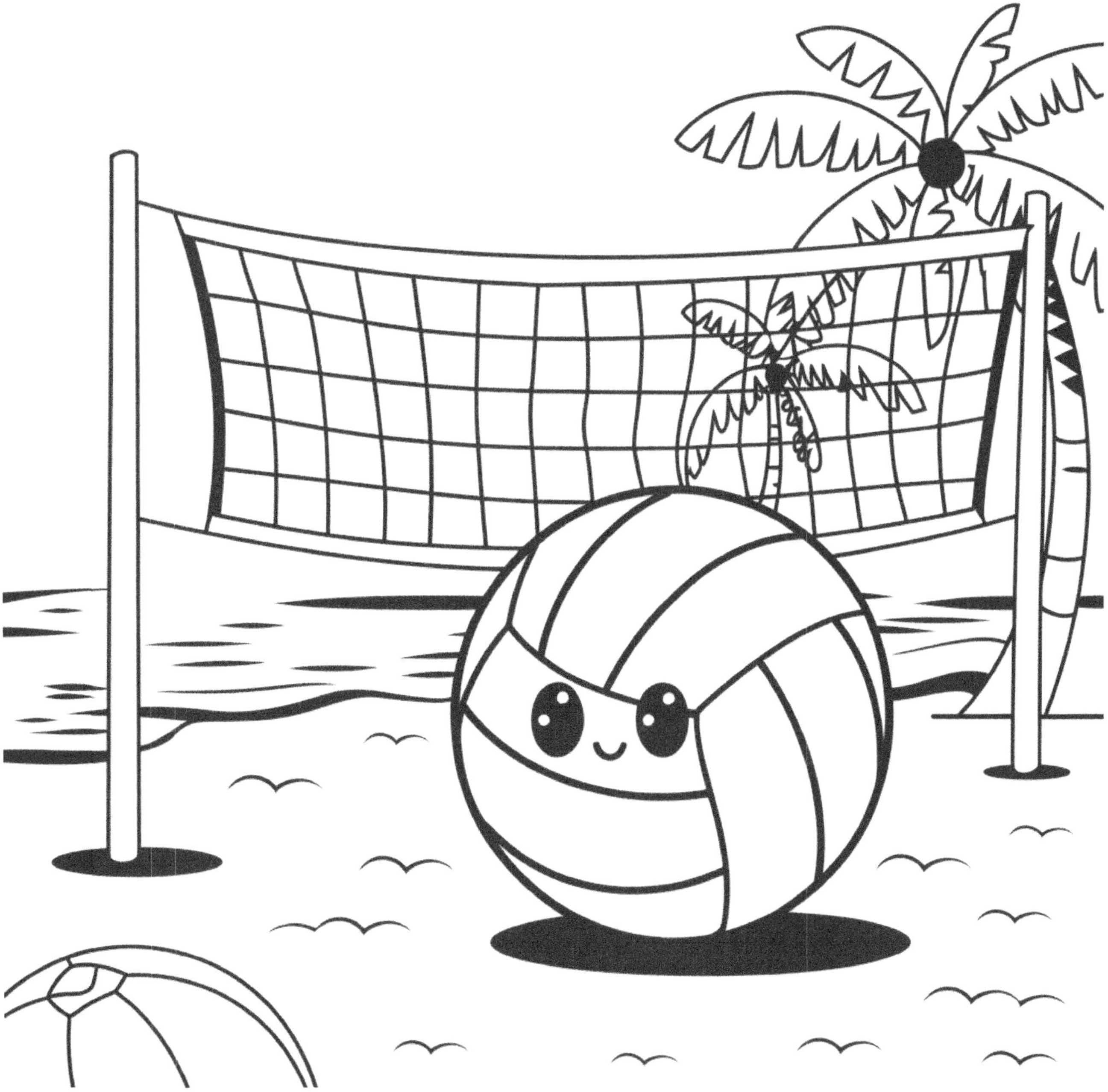

DOODLE

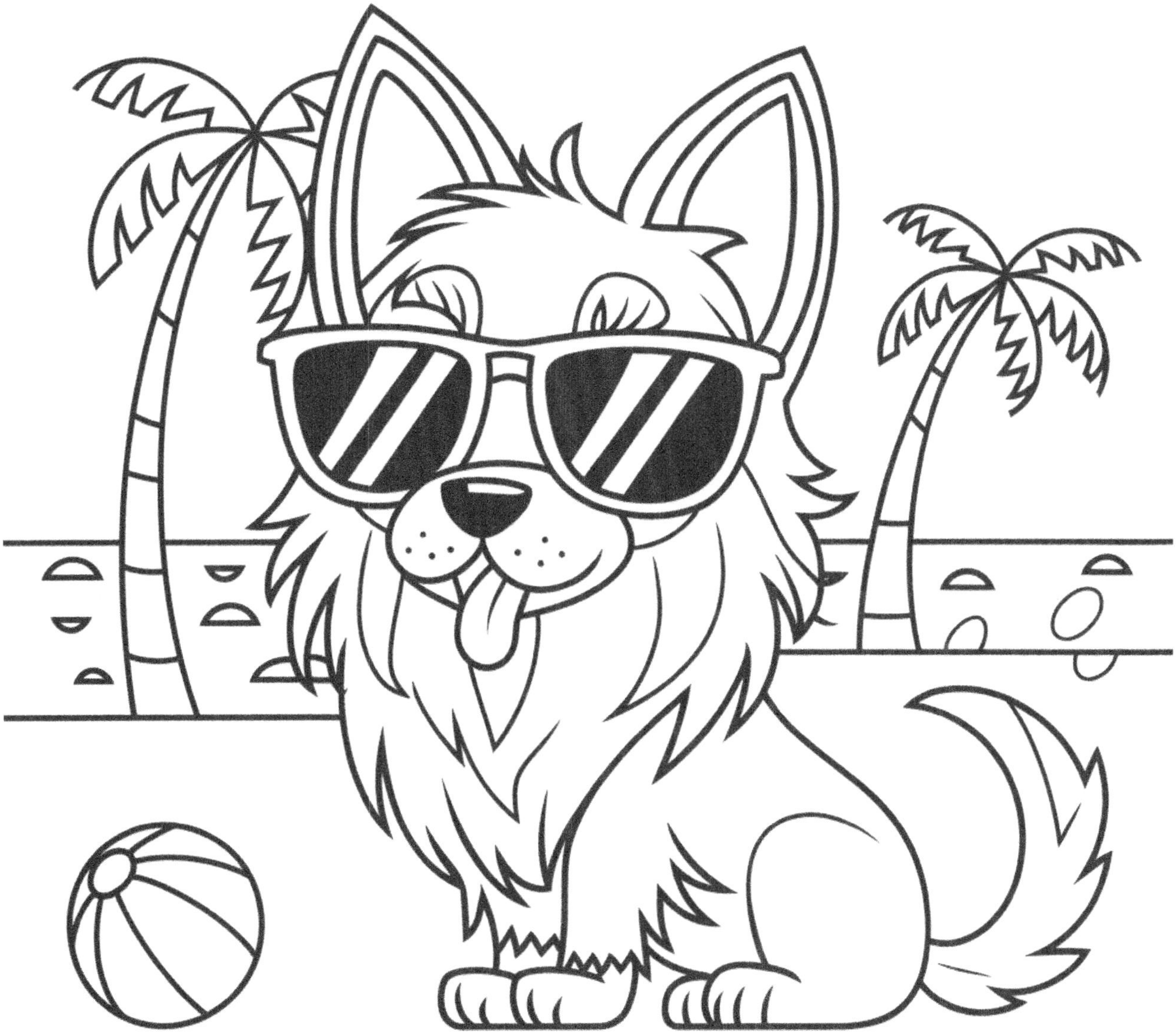

DOODLE

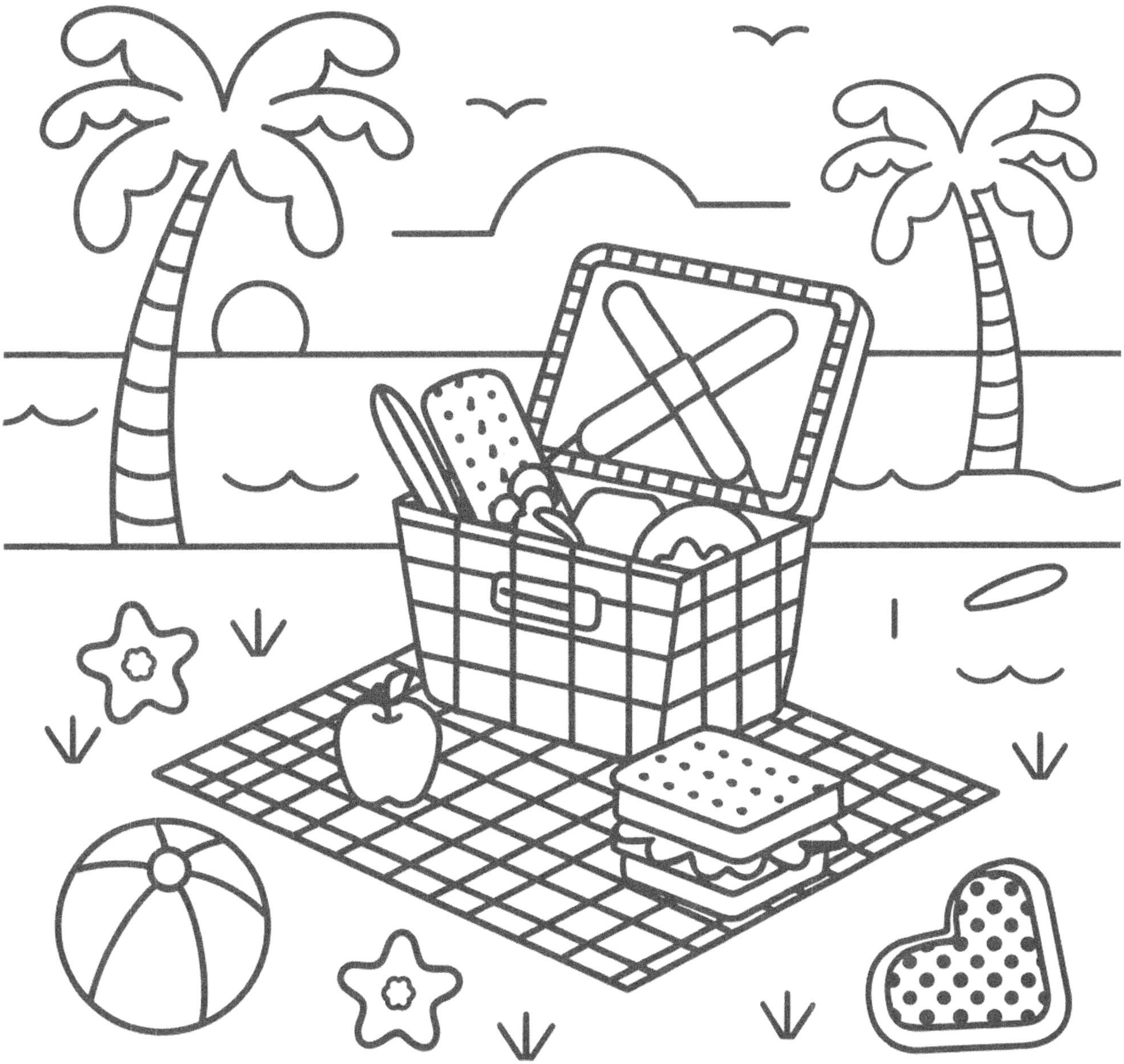

DOODLE

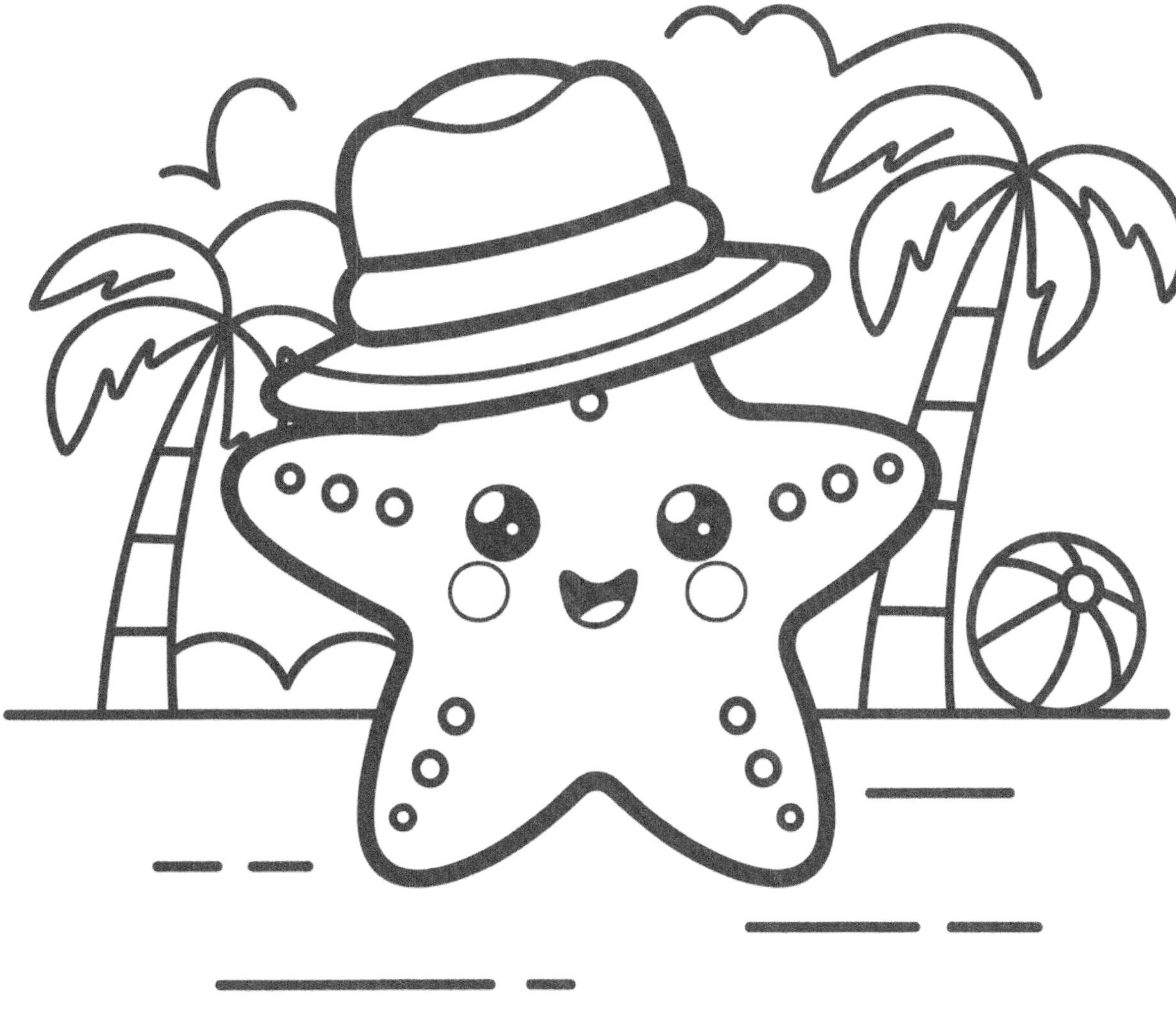

DOODLE

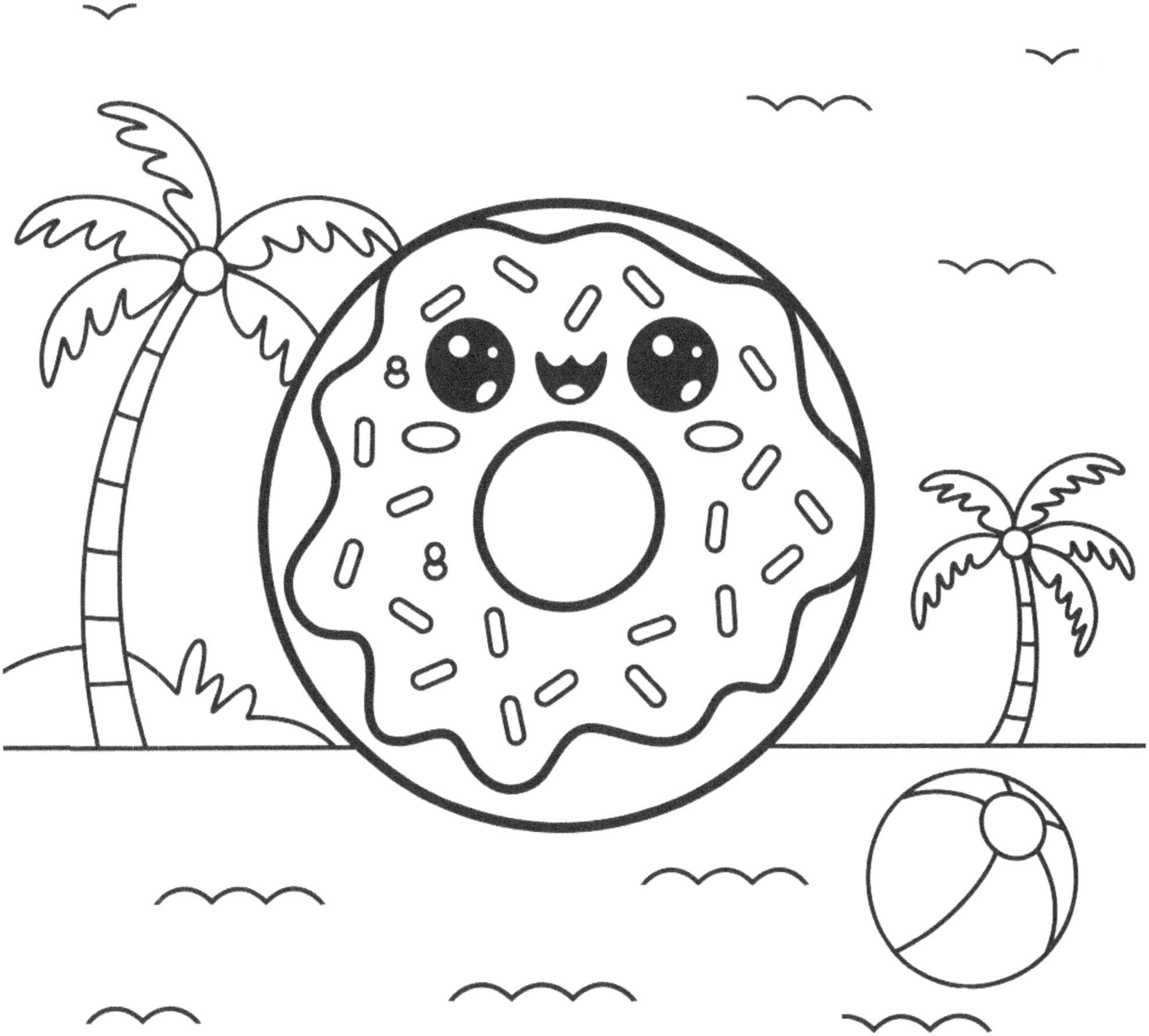

DOODLE

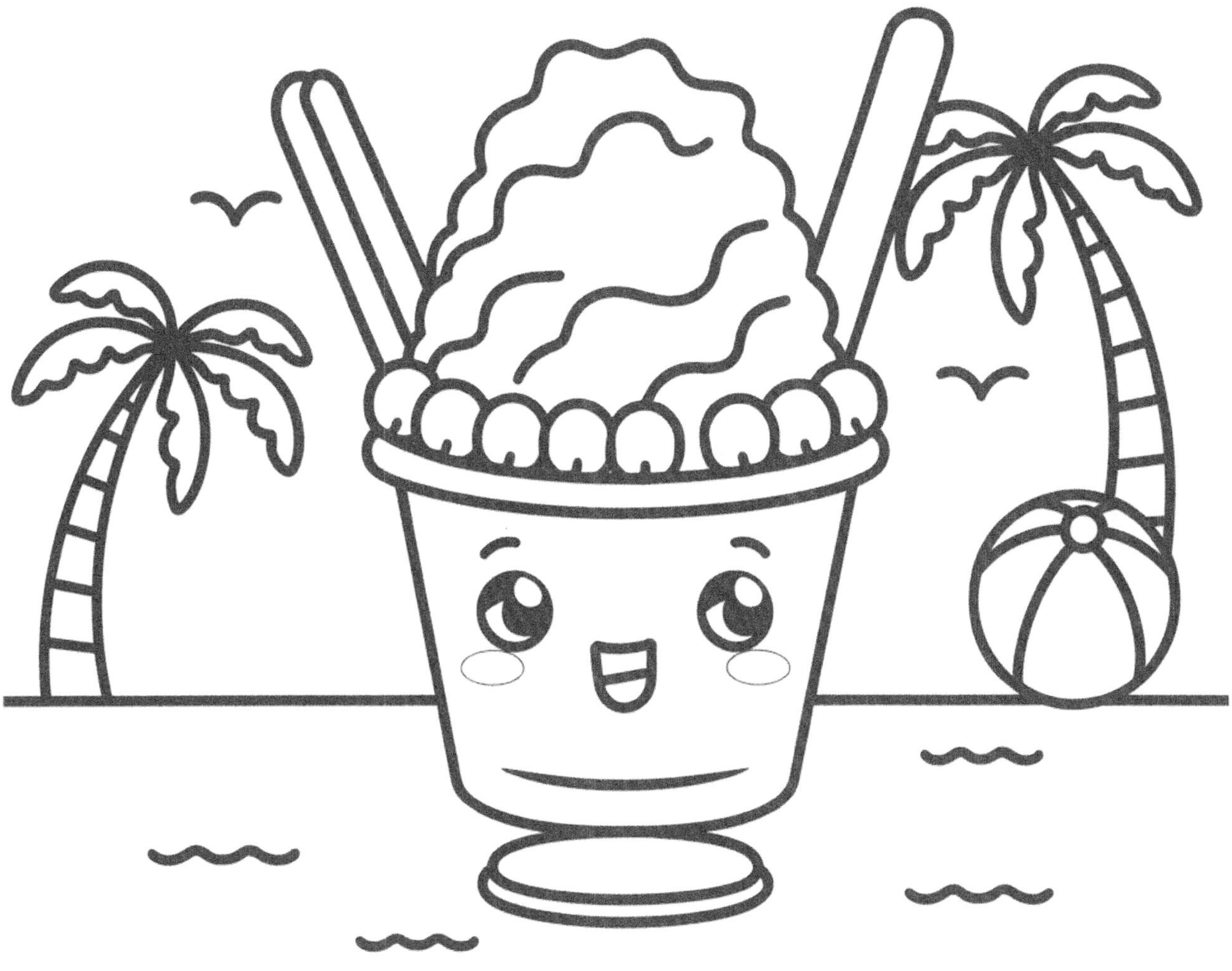

DOODLE

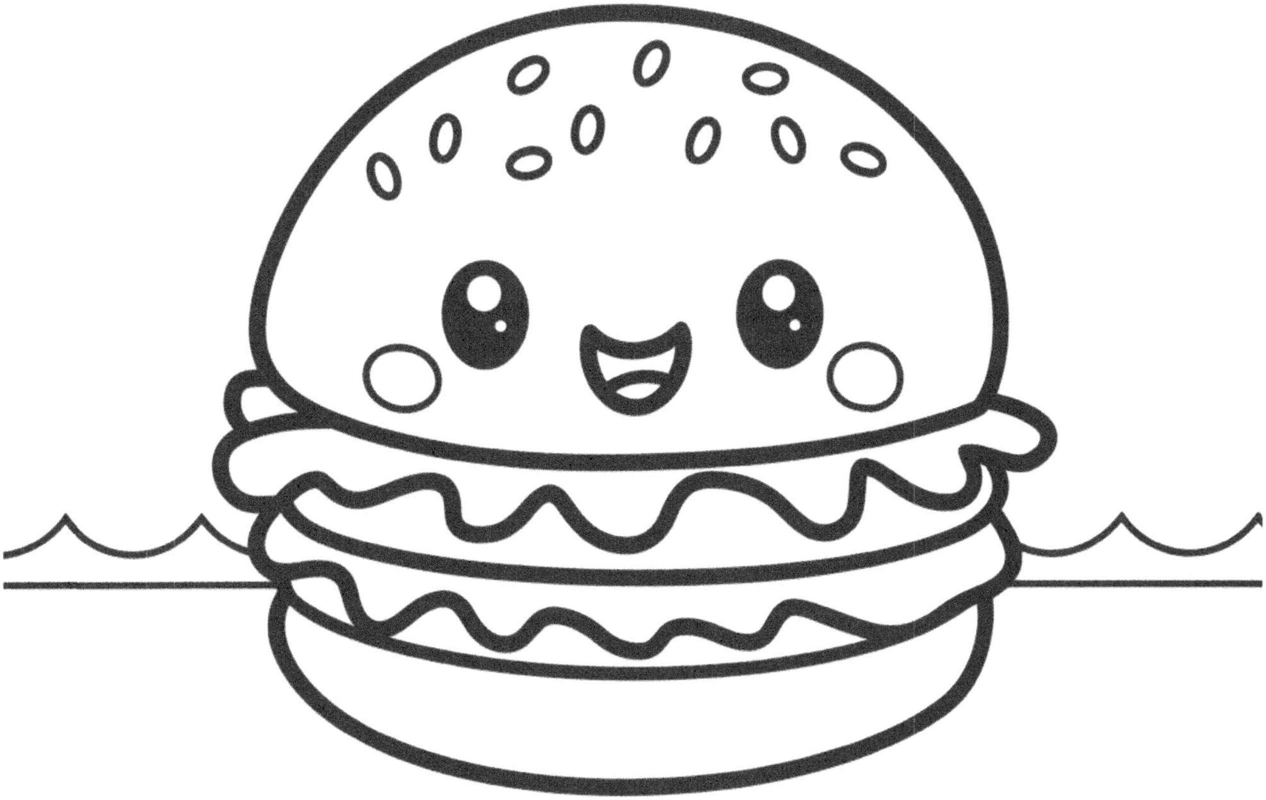

DOODLE

LUNCH BREAK

DOODLE

HAWAii

Made in the USA
Las Vegas, NV
30 April 2025